FIRST *and* SECOND SAMUEL

by

J. CARL LANEY

MOODY PRESS
CHICAGO

Library of Congress Cataloging in Publication Data

Laney, J. Carl, 1948-
   First and second Samuel.
   Bibliography: p. 129.
   1. Bible. O.T. Samuel—Commentaries. I. Title.

BS1325.3.L36   222'.407   81-18697

ISBN 0-8024-2010-9   AACR2

9 10 11 12 Printing/EP/Year 95 94 93 92 91

To
Mother and Dad,
who have instructed me
"in the good and right way"
(1 Samuel 12:23)

CONTENTS

CHAPTER   PAGE

Introduction   7

1. The Ministry of Samuel (1 Samuel 1-7)   15

2. The Reign of Saul (1 Samuel 8-15)   33

3. The Rise of David (1 Samuel 15-31)   54

4. The Triumphs of David (2 Samuel 1-10)   85

5. The Troubles of David (2 Samuel 11-20)   105

6. The Appendix to David's Career (2 Samuel 21-24)   122

Bibliography   131

INTRODUCTION

The books of Samuel record the historical drama of Israel's triumph and tragedy during the early period of the Hebrew monarchy. In the pages of these books we read of David's triumph over the Philistine Goliath. We also read of the tragedy of Saul's disobedience and David's immorality. The biblical record of Israel's beginnings as a political nation are masterfully recorded to give us not only an accurate historical document, but also to present significant spiritual lessons concerning the effects of sin, the workings of the Holy Spirit, and the sovereignty of God.

The goal of this commentary is to present a survey of First and Second Samuel. A synthesis of the early history of the Israelite monarchy will be presented; interpretive problems will be discussed; geographical references will be explained; theological issues will be considered; and biblical principles applicable to twentieth-century Christians will be presented. Ezra, a scribe skilled in the law of Moses, exemplifies the philosophy of Christian education that the readers of this commentary would be encouraged to emulate. "For Ezra had set his heart to *study* the law of the LORD, and to *practice* it, and to *teach* His statutes and ordinances in Israel" (Ezra 7:10, italics added).

TITLE

The two books of Samuel were originally one book, which was designated by the Masoretes as "The Book of Samuel." The translators of the Greek Septuagint brought Samuel and Kings together as a complete history of the monarchy and divided it into four sections called "Books of the Kingdoms." The Latin Vulgate later dropped the title "Books of the Kingdoms," shifted to the Hebrew division between Samuel and Kings, and gave the books the titles that western Christendom has employed ever since.

The twofold division of the books of Samuel was first introduced into the Hebrew text by the Venetian printer Daniel Bomberg in his first edition of the Hebrew Bible, dated 1516. The book is appropriately named after Samuel, the principal character of the early narratives, who played a prominent role in the anointing of Israel's first two kings, Saul and David.

AUTHOR

The books of Samuel are anonymous. Although the author is not named, suggested authors or coauthors include Abiathar, Nathan and Gad, and pupils from Samuel's school of the prophets. According to the Jewish Talmud, Samuel was the author of the first part of the book (chapters 1-24) and the remainder of First and Second Samuel was composed by Nathan and Gad as perhaps indicated in 1 Chronicles 29:29. The multiple authorship would in no way detract from the unity of the books in view of the supernatural moving of the Holy Spirit in the hearts and minds of the human authors (2 Peter 1:20-21).

DATE OF WRITING

There are indications that parts of the book were written after the death of Samuel (cf. 1 Sam. 25:1, 28:3) and perhaps even after the division of the kingdom (cf. 1 Sam. 27:6). However, since the book has no reference to the fall of Samaria, it is reasonable to assume that the writing was completed by 722 B.C. The eyewitness accounts, general antiquity of linguistic features, and authorship suggested by the Talmud indicate that the writing was done during David's day or shortly thereafter (c. 1025-900 B.C.).

HISTORICAL SETTING

The events of the books of Samuel cover the period from the ministry of Eli the high priest to the close of King David's reign. The conquest of Canaan by Joshua, around 1400 B.C., provided a homeland for the people of Israel. The judges had provided both spiritual and military leadership for the tempestuous three hundred years that followed. Now, in response to external political pressure, Israel was on the verge of establishing the monarchy. Taking 931 B.C. as the date of the division of the kingdom, the following dates for Israel's first three kings may be calculated:

Saul	40 years (cf. Acts 13:21)	1050-1010 B.C.
David	40 years (cf. 2 Sam. 5:4)	1010-970 B.C.
Solomon	40 years (cf. 1 Kings 11:42)	970-931 B.C.

Samuel's date of birth may be determined by the fact that he had sons old enough to be judges in Beersheba (1 Sam. 8:1-2) before Saul began to reign in 1050 B.C. That places Samuel's birth around 1100 B.C., just prior to the outbreak of Ammonite and Philistine oppression and the birth of Samson.

THE RELIGIOUS SCENE

The nation of Israel is seen to be at a religious low point as the narrative begins, for even the priesthood is corrupt (1 Sam. 2:12-17). Samuel's sons, who served as judges, were dishonest and corrupt (8:2-3), and the people of Israel were refusing to listen to the voice of their prophet Samuel (8:19). Yet in the midst of that corruption there was a righteous remnant of Israelites who were faithfully worshiping and sacrificing to the Lord at Shiloh (1:3). As this historical period begins, we find that the Ark of the Covenant is at Shiloh (4:4). It was later taken from there to the battle of Ebenezer, where it was captured by the Philistines (4:11). The Ark was later returned to Beth-shemesh (6:19) and then to Kiriath-jearim (7:1). It was eventually brought to Jerusalem by David twenty years later (2 Sam. 6).

THE POLITICAL SCENE

Politically, the book begins with the last judge, Samuel. The people of Israel refused to listen to Samuel as God's spokesman and wanted a king to rule over them (8:19). Samuel anointed Saul as Israel's first king (10:1) and later anointed David to succeed him (16:6-13). Gibeah (Tell el-Ful) was Saul's fortress and capital (10:26, 15:34). David reigned seven and a half years in Hebron before he moved his capital to Jerusalem after being appointed king over all Israel (2 Sam. 5:3-5).

THE INTERNATIONAL SCENE

Internationally, the period of the united monarchy was a time of transition. The great empires of the ancient world were in a state of weakness that allowed Israel to develop nationally without external restraint. The Hittites of Asia Minor had passed into insignificance. Assyria was in a state of decline. Egypt was weak and involved in internal conflict. The Philistines, having recently migrated from the Aegean Islands and Asia Minor (c. 1168 B.C.), constituted Israel's main threat during this period. The Philistines had a monopoly on iron that gave them a decided military and economic advantage and kept Israel on the defensive (c. 1 Sam. 13:19-22).

The threat of the Philistines was an impetus to the nation to unite under the leadership of Samuel, Saul, and David. The weakness of the great powers on the international scene made possible the expansion of the kingdom under David until Israel reached its peak of military and political power.

STATE OF THE TEXT

Although the books of Samuel are masterpieces in ancient historiography, some portions of the Hebrew text are found to be in a rather poor state of preservation. For example, there is the problem with the number preceding the word for *years* in 1 Samuel 13:1. Also in 1 Samuel 12:11 there is the problem with the name of the judge Bedan, probably a reference to Abdon (cf. Judg. 12:13) or possibly Barak (cf. Judg. 5:1). The exact reason the Masoretic text of Samuel has more difficulties than the text of other Old Testament books is not clear. Perhaps the copy used by the Masoretes, who standardized the Hebrew text (c. A.D. 600-950), was worm-eaten or frayed from overuse. Those problems, however, are not beyond solution. Fragments of Samuel found among the Dead Sea Scrolls indicate that the Hebrew underlying the Septuagint (LXX) was superior to the Masoretic tradition. Thus, the Septuagint is of great value in determining the correct readings of many difficult passages in the books of Samuel.

LITERARY FORM

While completing his doctoral dissertation at Brandeis University, Herbert M. Wolf discovered a remarkable parallel to the basic outline of 1 Samuel 15 through 2 Samuel 8 in the Hittite "Apology of Hattusilis," a thirteenth-century dynastic defense.[1] In that ancient document a king (or his supporters) outlines the reasons why his rule is legitimate. Such an apology would be particularly important in the case of a king who founded a new dynasty and might be charged with usurping the throne. That was the case both with Hattusilis and King David, who founded new dynasties. The "dynastic defense" includes the following elements or characteristics:

1. In the dynastic defense the disqualification of the preceding ruler is described in detail. That feature is readily observable in 1 Sam. 15, which records Saul's rejection as king by the Lord.

2. In the dynastic defense, great stress is placed upon the events that occur before the king's accession. The history develops to a climax when the hero is placed on the throne. That characteristic can be seen in 1 Samuel 16 through 2 Samuel 5, which records David's three anointings, exploits, and preparations for rule.

3. In the dynastic defense, emphasis is placed on the ability of the new king to lead and rule as evidenced by his military achievements. In 1 Samuel 17, which records David's slaying of Goliath, the new king is seen to be a man of tremendous military ability and potential for leadership.

4. A prominent characteristic of the king in the dynastic defense is his lenience toward political foes. Followers were not allowed to assassinate the ruling king, in contrast to the methods used by usurpers. In 1 Samuel 24 and 26 David is seen to have refused to slay Saul and prohibited his men from taking Saul's life.

5. The dynastic defense also shows how the new king, after coming to power, is very much interested in religious matters. In 2 Samuel 6 and 7 David is seen to be much concerned with the Ark, worship, and the blessing of the Lord.

6. The dynastic defense also includes a summary of the reign of the king, demonstrating the divine blessing on his rule as evidenced by the expansion of his kingdom and the establishment of peace with the surrounding nations. That feature is observed in 2 Samuel 8, where David's conquests are recounted.

In light of the impact of foreign cultures upon Israel in David's day, the similarities between the Apology of Hattusilis and 1 Samuel 15 to 2 Samuel 8 could hardly be mere coincidence. The literary form of 1 Samuel 15 to 2 Samuel 8 is of tremendous significance. A proper understanding of the dynastic defense assists the interpreter in explaining the purpose and arrangement of the events recorded in the biblical narrative.

PURPOSE

The historical purpose of the books of Samuel is to provide an official account of the ministry of Samuel along with the rise and development of the monarchy and the kingdom of Israel from the days of Saul through most of the reign of David. Theologically the books are intended to show the sovereignty of Yahweh over the theocratic ("God as ruler") kingdom as He sets up, deposes, and commands the leaders of Israel.

THEME

The unifying theme of Samuel is the establishment of the kingdom of Israel, progressing from a loosely connected group of Hebrew tribes to a solidified kingdom under David.

THEOLOGY

Although the books of Samuel are historically oriented, they also present some great biblical theology. Many important and practical truths are highlighted in this historical record.

THE THEOCRATIC KINGDOM

A *theocracy* is a government in which God rules as supreme monarch. God's program to manifest His sovereignty on earth may be called the "theocratic kingdom." It is the rule of God over His people through a divinely chosen representative who speaks and acts for Him. The administration of God's theocratic kingdom through divinely appointed kings is anticipated in several Old Testament passages (Gen. 17:5-7; 35:11; 49:10; Num. 24:17; and Deut. 17:14-20). The theocratic kingdom program is intended to manifest God's universal sovereignty as He sets up (1 Sam. 9:16-17), commands (1 Sam. 15:2-3), and deposes (1 Sam. 15:26, 28) the rulers of Israel.

THE WORKINGS OF THE SPIRIT

First Samuel provides a unique study of the workings of the

Holy Spirit in the Old Testament economy. The Spirit of Yahweh is seen to come upon Saul mightily for empowerment for his divinely appointed tasks (10:6, 10; 11:6). The Spirit of Yahweh also came upon David after his anointing by Samuel (16:3). That the Holy Spirit did not permanently indwell Old Testament believers is apparent from the fact that the Spirit of Yahweh is said to have departed from Saul (16:14; cf. Psalm 51:11). Although the indwelling of the Spirit in the Old Testament is selective and temporary, in the New Testament it is permanent and universal for all believers (cf. 1 Cor. 12:13; Rom. 8:9).

THE EFFECTS OF SIN

The books of Samuel are very instructive concerning the personal and national effects of sin. The sins of Eli and his sons resulted in their deaths (1 Sam. 2:12-17, 22-25; 3:10-14; 4:17-18). The lack of reverence for the Ark resulted in the deaths of a number of Israelites at Beth-shemesh (1 Sam. 6:19). Saul's sin and disobedience resulted in the judgment of being rejected by Yahweh as king over Israel (1 Sam. 13:9, 13-14; 15:8-9, 20-23). Saul's experience illustrates the principle that disobedience to God's Word may eliminate opportunities for service. Although David's sin with Bathsheba was confessed after Nathan's reproof and forgiven by the Lord (2 Sam. 12:1-13), David suffered the inevitable and devastating consequences of the sin (2 Sam. 12:11-14).

THE SOVEREIGNTY OF GOD

The sovereignty of God is clearly seen in the fact that it is God who selected both Saul and David to be king (1 Sam. 9:17; 16: 12-13). God's permissive will is evidenced by the fact that He allowed Israel to have a king even after warning the people against it (1 Sam. 8:10-22). Israel's error was in their attitude and timing (1 Sam. 8:5, 20). With respect to sin and evil, God wills to permit it (cf. Gen. 50:20; Acts 2:23) but not to effect it, for He is not the author of evil (James 1:13).

THE DAVIDIC COVENANT

Second Samuel records the Davidic Covenant (7:12-16), which amplifies and confirms the promise that God would make Abraham

a great nation (Gen. 12:2). In 2 Samuel 7:16 God promises David
and his posterity an eternal house, an eternal throne, and an eternal
kingdom. In essence, God guaranteed David that the right to rule
over Israel would always belong to one of his descendants. Luke
1:32-33 records that the Davidic Covenant will ultimately be
fulfilled in the person of Christ when He returns to reign over
David's kingdom.

OUTLINE

(First Samuel)

Section   *Chapter*

    1. The Ministry of Samuel   1-7
    2. The Reign of Saul   8-15
    3. The Rise of David   16-31

(Second Samuel)

    4. The Triumphs of David   1-10
    5. The Troubles of David   11-20
    6. The Appendix to David's Career   21-24

NOTES

1. Herbert Martin Wolf, "The Apology of Hattusilis Compared with Other
   Political Self-Justifications of the Ancient Near East" (Ph.D. diss.,
   Brandeis University, 1967), pp. 1-276.

1

THE MINISTRY OF SAMUEL

1 SAMUEL 1-7

THE BIRTH OF SAMUEL (1:1—2:11)
  Samuel's Family (1:1-8)
  Hannah's Vow (1:9-18)
  Hannah's Blessing (1:19-20)
  Hannah's Obedience (1:21-28)
  Hannah's Praise (2:1-11)

THE CORRUPTION OF THE PRIESTHOOD (2:12-36)
  The Sin of Eli's Sons (2:12-17)
  The Blessing on Hannah (2:18-21)
  The Immorality of Eli's Sons (2:22-26)
  The Prophecy Concerning Eli and His Sons (2:27-36)

THE CALL OF SAMUEL (3:1-21)
  Samuel's Call (3:1-18)
  Samuel's Ministry (3:19-21)

THE JUDGMENT ON ELI'S HOUSE (4:1-22)
  Israel's Defeat at Ebenezer (4:1-2)
  Israel's Superstitious Use of the Ark (4:3-9)
  Israel's Defeat and Loss of the Ark (4:10-22)

THE WANDERINGS OF THE ARK (5:1—7:2)
  From Ebenezer to Ashdod (5:1-7)
  From Ashdod to Gath (5:8-9)
  From Gath to Ekron (5:10—6:9)
  From Ekron to Beth-shemesh (6:10-20)
  From Beth-shemesh to Kiriath-jearim (6:21—7:2)

THE VICTORY OVER THE PHILISTINES (7:3-17)
  The Preparation for Battle (7:3-4)
  The Attainment of Victory (7:5-14)
  The Labors of Samuel (7:15-17)

1

THE MINISTRY OF SAMUEL

1 SAMUEL 1-7

The first seven chapters of the book introduce the prophet Samuel, probably the greatest Old Testament figure since Moses. Samuel is often considered the last of the judges (7:6, 15; 12:11) and the first of the prophets (3:20). He was of Levitical descent and served as a priest in Israel (10:8). Samuel is well-known as a great prophet of prayer. Again and again we see him interceding in behalf of the people of Israel (7:5; 8:6; 15:11). It was Samuel who said to the people of Israel, "Far be it from me that I should sin against the Lord by ceasing to pray for you" (12:23).

THE BIRTH OF SAMUEL (1:1-2—2:11)

Samuel was born during a time of Philistine oppression (4:1, 17), religious scandal (2:22), and limited prophetic influence (3:1). Samuel's birth, around 1100 b.c., may be viewed as a ray of hope at a time of impending disaster.

Samuel's Background (1:1-8)

Samuel was born into the family of a devout Levite residing in the hill country of Ephraim. Elkanah, whose name means "God has created," was a Levite by lineage, but not of the Aaronic priesthood (cf. 1 Chron. 6:26, 33). Elkanah's home town was Ramathaim-zophim ("the heights of the Zuphite"), which is a longer name for "Ramah" (1:19), a city that is probably to be identified with er-Ram, a site just five miles north of Jerusalem. The designation *Ephraimite* (1:1) refers to Elkanah's geographical situation in the territory of Ephraim, not his ancestry.

Elkanah was a polygamist. It was a marital situation that made for jealousy and strife in family relationships (cf. Gen. 30:1;

1 Sam. 1:6-7). Though at variance with God's ideal for marriage—one man with one woman (Gen. 2:24), polygamy was permitted by Old Testament law in the case of a childless first marriage (Deut. 21:15-17) and in the situation of Levirate marriage (Deut. 25:5-10). Elkanah probably took a second wife, Peninnah ("pearl"), because his first wife, Hannah ("grace"), was barren.

Elkanah's devotion to the Lord is evidenced by the fact of his regular yearly worship of "the LORD of hosts" at Shiloh (cf. Deut. 16:16). "The LORD (Yahweh) of hosts" is a military designation referring to God as the one who commands the angelic armies of heaven (1 Kings 22:19, Luke 2:13, Rev. 19:14) and the armies of Israel (1 Sam. 17:45). The term emphasizes the sovereignty and omnipotence of God (1:3). Shiloh, located twenty miles north of Jerusalem, was the religious center of the nation and location of the Tabernacle (Josh. 18:1) until its destruction after the loss of the Ark (1 Sam. 4).

Although Elkanah expressed his deep love for Hannah by giving her a double portion of the sacrifice, that did not compensate for her sense of loss in being unable to bear children. In ancient Israel barrenness was considered a tragic thing since the family name could not be carried on, and the woman would have no chance to become the mother of the Messiah. God's sovereignty over childbearing is expressed in the phrase "the LORD had closed her womb" (1:5-6). It is *God* who opens the womb (Gen. 30: 2, 22) and provides children (Gen. 33:5; Psalm 127:3). Women today who have been unable to bear children should realize that: (1) God may still be preparing them to be mothers, (2) God may be preparing them to become foster or perhaps adoptive mothers, or (3) God's will may be that they not have children in order to be available to serve Him in some special way that would be otherwise impossible. Although Peninnah provoked Hannah, Elkanah encouraged her. He suggested that his love and care for Hannah was a greater blessing than having "ten sons"—a very large family (1:8).

Hannah's Vow (1:9-18)

Hannah makes an excellent biographical study for a Mother's Day message. She is an example of a mother devoted to God and to her family. Hannah also gave us an example of fervent prayer. There at Shiloh at one of the yearly feasts Hannah visited the Tabernacle and poured out her heart to the Lord. The phrase, "greatly distressed" (literally, "bitter of soul"), is descriptive of Hannah's emotional condition—disappointed and distressed over her inability to bear children (1:10). The essence of Hannah's prayer is her petition, "Remember me!" (1:11). Within her prayer Hannah made a vow to God—a vow that could have been annulled by Elkanah when he discovered what she had promised (cf. Num. 30:10-12). Hannah vowed that if God would give her a son, the child would be dedicated to lifelong Levitical service (cf. Num. 4:3; 8:24-26) and become a lifelong Nazirite (Num. 6:3-6). Her son would begin his Levitical service as a child and would always refrain from wine, haircuts, and ceremonial defilement.

Verses 12-16 are a sad commentary on the spiritual state of Israel at that time. When Eli, the high priest, saw Hannah praying fervently he assumed that she must be *drunk* (1:14). Hannah's response, "I have poured out my soul before the Lord," is an excellent description of fervent prayer (cf. Psalm 62:8, Phil. 4:6-7, 1 Pet. 5:7). The expression "a worthless woman" is literally "a daughter of Belial" (1:16). The Hebrew *belial* means "without value" and was used in later Jewish writings as a proper name for Satan (cf. The Book of Jubilees i.20; 2 Cor. 6:15).

After hearing Hannah's explanation Eli blessed her ("Go in peace") and prayed that God would grant her the petition. Having bared her heart before the Lord, Hannah experienced peace (cf. Phil. 4:6-7). She was able to eat, and her countenance was changed (1:18).

Hannah's Blessing (1:19-20)

God remembered Hannah, as she had requested (1:11, 19), and answered her prayer. The expression *knew* (KJV*) is a euphemism for sexual relations. When Hannah gave birth she named the child Samuel explaining, "Because I have asked him of the Lord" (1:20). Keil and Delitzsch interpret the name to mean "heard of God," commemorating the answer to prayer.[1] However, Brown, Driver, and Briggs's Hebrew lexicon explains the name as meaning "name of God" (*shem-El*), serving as a continual reminder of God's

*King James Version.

mercy toward those who call upon His name.[2] With that second view the majority of commentators concur.

Hannah's Obedience (1:21-28)

How easy it might have been for Hannah to rationalize her way out of keeping her vow. She could have argued that she had made a rash promise under severe emotional stress. But Hannah recognized the priority of obedience and the importance of keeping her vow (cf. Eccles. 5:4-5). Hannah did not go up to Shiloh to worship with her husband for several years until she had weaned the child and could fulfill her vow. Hebrew children were normally weaned from their mothers at two to three years of age (The apocryphal 2 Maccabees 7:27 makes reference to that fact). The word translated "weaned" literally means "dealt fully with" and may include the idea of spiritual training as well. It may well be that Samuel learned of the importance of prayer from his godly mother at a very young age and thus became a great prophet of prayer.

Old Testament law provided for a burnt offering to be given at the fulfillment of a special vow to the Lord (cf. Num. 15:3, 8). After offering the appropriate sacrifices (1:24-25), Hannah identified herself to Eli the priest and presented her child, Samuel, to the Lord. That was not "baby dedication" as might be inferred from the *New American Standard Bible*. Nor was the idea that of "loaning" the baby to God (KJV). The word for "dedicated" is literally translated "made him over to." The idea is that of a complete and irrevocable giving up of the child to the Lord. Hannah subjected her maternal instincts to her spiritual commitment and was careful to pay her vow even at great cost. The phrase "he worshiped" describes the response of Elkanah (1:28). His commitment to God is evidenced by the fact that he did not annul Hannah's vow according to the provisions of Numbers 30:10-14.

Hannah's Praise (2:1-11)

The scene recorded here stands in sharp contrast with the situation in 1:9-15 when Hannah was last at the Tabernacle. Here she rejoiced and praised God. Hannah's praise was in response to God's answer to her prayer and may have been delivered as a personal testimony before the congregation of worshipers at the Tabernacle. Like the psalms, this prayer is recorded as Hebrew poetry. The theme of Hannah's praise is her confidence in God's sovereignty over every aspect of life. Hannah also praised God for His holiness (2:2), knowledge (2:3), power (2:8), and judgment (2:10).

1. *Hannah's rejoicing* (2:1-2)

Hannah began her prayer with great rejoicing for being divinely delivered from barrenness. In doing so she recognized the unique holiness of Yahweh. The "horn" is an image of invincible strength (cf. Dan. 7:21; Zech. 1:18-21).

2. *Hannah's warning* (2:3)

Could verse 3 have possibly been addressed to Peninnah, Hannah's rival (cf. 1:6-7)?

3. *Hannah's testimony* (2:4-8)

Hannah proceeded to testify from her own experience how God intervenes in human affairs. A sovereign God can and does reverse human circumstances, humbling the proud and exalting the humble (2:7-8). Verse 6 points to the fact that the issues of life and death are in the hand of God. The Hebrew word *Sheol*, suitably translated "grave" in the King James Version, refers to a dark, shadowy, silent place of continued existence after death (Job 10:21-22; Psalms 94:17, 143:3). It appears that the word most often refers simply to the place of the dead—the grave of both the righteous and the wicked (cf. Gen. 37:35; Psalm 9:17).[3] However, Sheol can also be used in a more technical sense of the place of punishment for the wicked dead awaiting resurrection and final judgment (Num. 16:33; Job 24:19; Psalm 30:9; Isa. 38:18). In this latter sense it would be the equivalent of "hades" in the New Testament.

4. *Hannah's confidence* (2:9-11)

Hannah concluded by expressing her supreme confidence in God's power to protect and preserve His own. The righteous will be preserved, and the wicked will be punished. Having testified of God's blessing in her life Hannah returned home to Ramah, leaving Samuel to minister with Eli at Shiloh.

THE CORRUPTION OF THE PRIESTHOOD (2:12-36)

The rest of chapter 2 records the corruption of the priesthood in the time of Samuel resulting from Eli's failure to discipline his sons (3:13). Eli's sons dishonored God by despising His offerings and committing immorality with the women who served at the Tabernacle (2:17, 22).

The Sin of Eli's Sons (2:12-17)

The sons of Eli are described as "worthless men" (literally "sons of Belial"), an expression associated with idolatry and sensuality (Deut. 13:13; Judg. 19:22; 20:13). In addition, it is said that they did not "know" Yahweh. The word *know* speaks of an experiential, personal knowledge. How tragic to know about God, yet not know Him personally! It was the custom of Eli's sons to steal from God by taking any part of the sacrifice they desired, rather than their allotted portion (Lev. 7:34) and demanding the meat from the people before the fat had been burned as an offering to God (Lev. 3:3, 5). In essence, they disdained the offering of God, treating it irreverently and disrespectfully (2:17).

The Blessing on Hannah (2:18-21)

The conduct of Eli's sons is set in sharp contrast with the remarkable piety exhibited by Elkanah's family. Samuel was busy serving the Lord (2:18), and Hannah was ministering to the needs of her family (2:19). The linen ephod worn by Samuel was a close fitting, sleeveless outer vest extending to the hips and worn almost exclusively by priests, especially when officiating before the altar (Exod. 28:6-14; 1 Sam. 2:28). Hannah's obedience and devotion to God resulted in great blessing. Not only did God give her three more sons and two daughters, but she also had the privilege of watching her first-born, Samuel, grow before the Lord (2:21).

The Immorality of Eli's Sons (2:22-26)

Not only did Eli's sons steal from God, but they also committed adultery openly with the women who served at the Tabernacle (2:22; 4:19). The women mentioned here and in Exodus 38:8 were probably responsible for keeping the entrance of the Tabernacle clean. The Hebrew text of verse 24 suggests that the sin of those religious leaders was leading the people of Israel to transgress. The words "the LORD's people circulating" are better translated "causing the LORD's people to transgress." Although Eli warned his sons of the certain divine judgment for their sin, they would not listen. The preposition *for* (2:25) may denote result (i.e., "therefore the Lord . . ."), pointing to the severe consequence of their sin against God. In contrast to the apostate sons of Eli, Hannah's son was maturing both spiritually and socially (cf. Luke 2:52).

The Prophecy Concerning Eli and His Sons (2:26-36)

Chapter 2 concludes with a warning given to Eli concerning the impending divine judgment on his house and family. The rebuke was delivered by a "man of God," an unidentified prophet, or spokesman for the Lord. The essence of Eli's sin was that by neglecting his responsibility for child discipline, he actually esteemed his sons above the Lord (2:29). Although he warned his sons of divine judgment (2:25), he never rebuked them for their sins (3:13). Verse 30 sets forth the principle that with God, honor is reciprocal. God will honor those who honor Him. But note carefully that the reverse is also true.

The prophet predicted the destruction of the priestly family of Eli (2:31-34). That judgment was partially fulfilled in the massacre of the priests of Nob (cf. 1 Sam. 22:11-19) and ultimately fulfilled in the transfer of the priesthood to the family of Zadok in the time of Solomon (1 Kings 2:26-27, 35). The death of Eli's two sons, Hophni and Phinehas, on the same day would serve as a sign to validate the prophecy.

With the destruction of Eli's family God promised to raise up a faithful priest who will fulfill His will and whose house will endure. Although that priest has been identified as Samuel, or even Christ, it is preferable to view the prophecy as fulfilled in the accession of Zadok and his family to the priestly office in the time of Solomon (cf. 1 Kings 1:7-8; 2:26-27, 35).[4] Zadok himself served David and Solomon; his sons will serve in the millennial Temple (Ezek. 44:15; 48:11). The impoverishment predicted in verse 36 was probably fulfilled when Abiathar, a descendant of Eli, was dismissed from the priesthood by Solomon (1 Kings 2:27).

THE CALL OF SAMUEL (3:1-21)

Although Abraham was the first prophet (Gen. 20:7) and Moses was the greatest prophet (Deut. 18:15, 18-22; 34:10), Samuel was the first of a series of prophets called by the Lord to speak His Word to the people of Israel.

Samuel's Call (3:1-18)

Samuel was probably a young teenager when he was called to his prophetic ministry. The word translated "boy" means "young person" and is used of David when he slew Goliath (17:33). This was a time of extremely limited prophetic activity (3:1), probably because there were so few faithful men through whom God could deliver His Word. It was just before dawn while the golden lampstand before the veil was still burning (cf. Lev. 24:3; Exod. 27:20-21) that Samuel was called to his prophetic ministry. Three times he mistook God's voice for the voice of Eli. Verse 7 explains why. Although Samuel had been assisting Eli in the Tabernacle, he did not yet know the Lord in a personal way nor had he ever received God's Word by divine revelation. Finally Eli realized that it must be the Lord and instructed Samuel in an appropriate response (3:9).

When God spoke a fourth time Samuel responded, "Speak, for Thy servant is listening" (1 Sam. 3:10). The word translated "listening" means "to hear with interest" and can be translated "obey." Samuel was listening to God's word and was determined to obey it. Samuel exemplifies the kind of person that God can use—one who is always ready to receive God's message and obey His Word. The message God gave Samuel was an ear-tingling announcement of the impending destruction of Eli's house (3:11-14). The message spoken earlier by the "man of God" (2:30-34) was about to be fulfilled.

Eli's family was apparently guilty of "a sin of the high hand" (cf. Num. 15:30-31). For such defiant sin there was no atonement, and the death penalty would be immediately applied (2:33; 3:14).

Perhaps this is an Old Testament example of a kind of sin that is "unto death" (1 John 5:16-17). Samuel's first great test as a prophet of God was whether he would report the whole truth to Eli or compromise the message. He passed the test by speaking the whole counsel of the Lord concerning Eli and his family (3:17-18). Eli expressed no doubt that Yahweh had spoken through Samuel and submitted to God's sovereign discipline.

Samuel's Ministry (3:19-21)

Samuel's commitment to communicate God's truth brought him great blessing. God was with him and allowed none of his prophecies to go unfulfilled—literally, "to fall to the ground" (3:19). Soon Samuel became recognized by all Israel as God's spokesman. The expression "from Dan even to Beersheba" denotes the whole territory of Israel from its most northern to its most southern extremity—a distance of about 150 miles (cf. Judg. 20:1). Samuel's call to the prophetic ministry provided a basis for God's continued revealing of His will and word at Shiloh (3:21).

THE JUDGMENT ON ELI'S HOUSE (4:1-22)

First Samuel 4 records the fulfillment of the prophetic judgment to fall on Eli's family. The judgment came about as a result of a Philistine attack against Israel.

Israel's Defeat at Ebenezer (4:1-2)

The Philistines, commonly referred to in Egyptian texts as the "Sea Peoples," were Indo-Europeans who migrated from the Aegean Islands (cf. Amos 9:7) and Asia Minor to the eastern Mediterranean coastal region in the twelfth century B.C. Most scholars agree that they set out for Palestine and Egypt under the pressure of the invasion of the Dorian Greeks. Migrations of that kind had occurred earlier, for we see that Abraham had contact with "Philistines" as early as 2000 B.C. (Gen. 21:22-33). Although the early migrants were more peaceful, the later ones were very aggressive. Their invasion toppled many of the kingdoms of the ancient East. Rameses III (1198-1166 B.C.) boasts that he succeeded in repulsing the invasion, but as a result of the attack Egypt lost control of the southern coastal plain of Palestine, and there the

Philistines settled. They formed a very strong political and military organization with fortress cities at Ashkelon, Ashdod, Ekron, Gath, and Gaza. The Philistines soon became the greatest threat to Israelite security.

The battle between the Israelites and Philistines recorded here took place between Aphek and Ebenezer. Aphek, just eleven miles northeast of Joppa, was a strategic border city at the northern edge of the Philistine territory. Ebenezer, yet unidentified, was probably situated on the plain between Aphek and the hills to the west. The name *Ebenezer* ("stone of help") was given to commemorate Israel's victory at the site some twenty years later (cf. 7:12). The battle between Aphek and Ebenezer resulted in Israel's defeat and the loss of four thousand Israelite warriors (4:2).

Israel's Superstitious Use of the Ark (4:3-9)

The leaders of Israel quickly recognized the hand of the Lord in the outcome of the battle. In order to insure a future victory against the Philistines they determined to remove the Ark from the Tabernacle in Shiloh and take it with them into battle.

A twofold theological error lay at the basis of that plan. First, Israel failed to distinguish between the Ark as the symbol of God's presence (Exod. 25:22; 2 Sam. 6:2; Psalm 80:1), and the actual presence of God. It was the custom of ancient warriors to take their idols into battle so that their gods would deliver them (cf. 2 Sam. 5:21; 1 Chron. 14:12). That was apparently Israel's plan. Their error was in failing to recognize that God is omnipresent—not subject to spatial limitations (Psalm 139:7-10; Jer. 23:23-24). God would be with Israel in battle even when the Ark was in Shiloh. Second, Israel became superstitious about the Ark, believing divine power to be in the Ark itself rather than God. They viewed the Ark as a "lucky rabbit's foot" or good-luck charm that would insure their success in battle. Their error was in failing to recognize that God is omnipotent—infinite in power (Psalm 115:3; Jer. 32:17). Rather than placing their confidence in the Ark, the Israelites should have placed their faith in the infinite, all-powerful God. The two sons of Eli, Hophni and Phinehas, accompanied the Ark to the Israelite camp (4:4-5).

The joyful shouting of the Israelites at the sight of the Ark brought fear into the hearts of the Philistines (4:6-7). They clearly looked upon the Ark as some sort of idol—an Israelite god—and were stricken with fear. They had heard of what Israel's God had accomplished for His people at the Exodus (4:8).

Israel's Defeat and Loss of the Ark (4:10-22)

The Israelites were again defeated at the hands of the Philistines, and this time thirty thousand Israelite warriors were slain in battle. One soldier who escaped from the battlefield ran up the Shiloh Valley to bring a report of Israel's defeat to Eli. He reported Israel's defeat, the death of Eli's sons, and worse yet, the capture of the Ark by the Philistines (4:17). When Eli heard that the Ark had been taken he fell off his seat by the gate and broke his neck. God was beginning to destroy the apostate house of Eli so He could replace it with a family of faithful priests (2:33-36).

Upon hearing the news of the death of her husband and father-in-law and that the Ark had been captured, Phinehas's wife went into labor and delivered a son. Like Rachel (Gen. 35:16-20), she died in childbirth, but before her death she named the child. His name would be Ichabod—literally, "no glory," for the loss of the Ark meant the absence of glory in Israel (4:22).

It is probable that the Ark never returned to Shiloh, for archaeological excavation indicates that the city was destroyed around 1050 B.C.[5] It may have been destroyed by the Philistines after they captured the Ark. Jeremiah 7:12 reveals that the Lord brought about the destruction of Shiloh as a judgment on His wicked people.

THE WANDERINGS OF THE ARK (5:1–7:2)

The next several chapters of 1 Samuel record the wanderings of the Ark and the havoc it caused the Philistines while it was in their possession. One spiritual lesson to be gleaned from this section is that whatever is acquired by improper means can never bring blessing.

From Ebenezer to Ashdod (5:1-7)

The Ark was first taken to Ashdod, a Philistine city located on the Mediterranean coast about twenty-two miles south of Joppa.

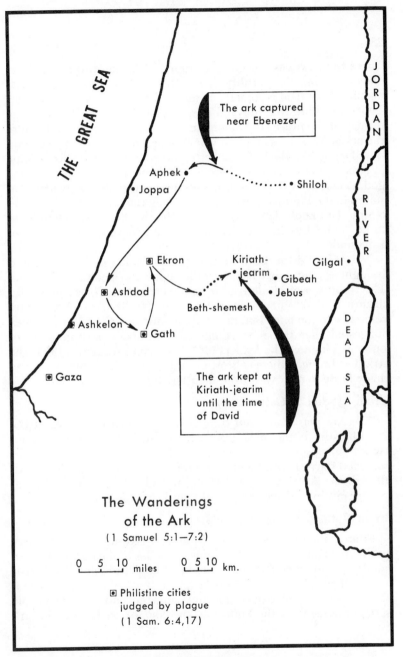

THE GREAT SEA

JORDAN RIVER

The ark captured
near Ebenezer

Aphek •
• Joppa
• Shiloh

◉ Ekron
Kiriath-
jearim
Gilgal •
• Gibeah
• Jebus

◉ Ashdod
Beth-shemesh

◉ Ashkelon
◉ Gath

DEAD SEA

◉ Gaza

The ark kept at
Kiriath-jearim
until the time
of David

The Wanderings
of the Ark
(1 Samuel 5:1—7:2)

0   5   10 miles   0 5 10 km.

◉ Philistine cities
judged by plague
(1 Sam. 6:4,17)

Fig. 1.1

There the Ark was placed as a trophy of battle in the temple of Dagon, a Philistine fertility deity. In Ugaritic literature, the Canaanite deity Baal is sometimes referred to as the "son of Dagon." Twice the Philistine idol fell down before the Ark. Imagine the dismay of the priests of Dagon, finding their idol prostrated before the ark of Yahweh as though worshiping Israel's God. The second time Dagon fell, the idol was destroyed (5:3-4). That was a divine judgment and is recorded here as a polemic against the Philistine god. Verse 5 explains, in a humorous vein, that this incident resulted in the Philistine custom of avoiding the threshold of Dagon's temple (cf. Zeph. 1:9). Apparently the threshold was considered to be "holy" by virtue of its contact with the head and hands of Dagon.

Not only did the Lord destroy the Philistine idol, but He also brought a plague of "hemorrhoids" upon the people of Ashdod. The Hebrew word is derived from the verb *to swell,* and may refer to any kind of tumors or, perhaps, boils. In light of the later reference to the mice that ravaged the land (cf. 6:4-5), it has been suggested that those "swellings" were buboes, symptomatic of bubonic plague. The leaders of Ashdod soon recognized that the Ark had brought them misfortune rather than blessing, and they made haste to remove it from their territory.

From Ashdod to Gath (5:8-9)

The Ark was transfered from Ashdod to Gath, another of the five Philistine cities (6:17), probably located at Tell es-Safi, about twelve miles southeast of Ashdod. The divine plague, of course, followed the Ark, producing sores on both the young and old. Although the Ark was a good thing, it had been acquired by improper means and therefore could not bring blessing.

From Gath to Ekron (5:10—6:9)

From Gath the Ark was transferred to Ekron, a Philistine city probably located at Tell Miqne, just six miles to the north. There a similar plague resulted, and the Philistine people decided that it was in their own best interests to return the Ark to Israel (5:11).

After seven months of plague and panic the leaders of the people sought advice from the Philistine "theologians" as to how the Ark should be restored to Israelite possession (6:2). The priests and diviners warned against returning the Ark empty and counseled that an offering would be necessary to appease the God of Israel and bring an end to the plague. A guilt offering of five golden hemorrhoids and five golden mice was prepared—one of each for the five Philistine cities (6:4, 17-18). A new cart was built to carry the Ark back to Israelite territory. The cart was to be pulled by two "milch cows"—cows still nursing their young (6:7). For nursing cows to leave their young and make a beeline for the Israelite city of Beth-shemesh would be quite unusual. That would be a clear indication that the cows were being led supernaturally and that the plague had indeed been the judgment of Yahweh (6:9).

From Ekron to Beth-shemesh (6:10-20)

The Ark was dispatched from Ekron, and the cows pulling the cart headed straight for Beth-shemesh (Tell er-Rumeileh), a Levitical city (Josh. 21:16) in the Sorek Valley about eight miles east of Ekron. The Israelites reaping wheat in the fields of Beth-shemesh were the first to see the Ark, and they thanked God for its safe return by offering the two milch cows as a burnt offering. Although there is no indication that the Ark was in Ashkelon (nine and a half miles south of Ashdod) or Gaza (twelve miles south of Ashkelon), they apparently came under the plague that fell on all the Philistines (cf. 6:4).

An unfortunate tragedy took place at Beth-shemesh with the return of the Ark. The Lord slew some of the men of Beth-shemesh who were guilty of the presumptuous sin of gazing into the Ark, apparently a violation of Numbers 4:20 (cf. Num. 4:5-6, 15-20). The Ark was a holy object and not to be meddled with by the unconsecrated. The number 50,070 is doubted even by conservative scholars and probably represents a scribal error in transmission.[6] Since the number fifty thousand is absent in three Hebrew manuscripts, the correct figure is probably seventy as recorded by Josephus (*Antiquities* VI. 16).

From Beth-shemesh to Kiriath-jearim (6:21—7:2)

So disturbed were the people of Beth-shemesh by the tragedy that had befallen them that they requested the men of Kiriath-jearim to come and remove the Ark from their valley. The Ark was then taken to the house of Abinadab in Kiriath-jearim, identified with Deir el-Azar, just ten miles west of Jerusalem. There Eleazar, of no apparent priestly descent, was consecrated (literally "set apart") to care for the Ark. The Ark of the Covenant remained at Kiriath-jearim for at least twenty years until David brought it to Jerusalem (2 Sam. 6:2-3). Since the "twenty years" (7:2) does not bring us to the time of David and the events of 2 Samuel 6, it must refer to the period until some important event—perhaps the repentance recorded in 7:3-4.

THE VICTORY OVER THE PHILISTINES (7:3-17)

The rest of chapter seven records Israel's third major battle with the Philistines during the ministry of Samuel. This time the Israelites were victorious. The victory resulted from Israel's repentance and was accomplished by God's power.

The Preparation for Battle (7:3-4)

Before Israel's third confrontation with the Philistines, Samuel gave them the key to victory. He declared that repentance from idolatry and loyalty toward God were the prerequisites for blessing (7:3). Spiritual victory is the necessary prelude to success in every area of life (cf. Josh. 1:8). The people of Israel responded by putting away the idols of the Canaanite deities Baal and Ashtaroth. Idols of that sort and many other cult objects can be seen in Israel's museums today. Baal was the supreme male deity of the Phoenician and Canaanite nations. He was a fertility god whose domain was the sky. From there he fertilized the land and thus controlled nature. Ashtaroth (7:3-4; 12:10; 31:10) is the plural form of "Ashtoreth," the Canaanite mother goddess of fertility, love, and war. The rites connected with her worship were of a very licentious nature and usually involved prostitution. Ashtoreth was the supreme goddess of Canaan and the female companion of Baal.

The Attainment of Victory (7:5-14)

Before the battle against the Philistines, Samuel gathered the people of Israel together at Mizpah (Tell en-Nasbeh), seven miles north of Jerusalem, for a prayer meeting. There they demonstrated their repentance by pouring out water (a sign of repentance, cf. Psalm 62:8, Lam. 2:19), fasting, and confessing their sin. The Philistines noted the renewed unity and commitment among the Israelites and considered it a threat to their security. They immediately organized an attack on Israel (7:7).

While Samuel was sacrificing and praying to the Lord, the Philistines engaged the Israelite army in battle (7:8-10). The Lord graciously intervened in behalf of His repentant people and caused a great thunder to confuse the Philistines enabling the Israelites to achieve a tremendous victory. As a result, Israel was able to receive back their territory from the Philistines as far west (i.e., exclusive of) as Ekron and Gath (7:13-14). To commemorate the victory and acknowledge the Lord's help, Samuel set up a memorial stone on the battlefield and named it *Ebenezer*, meaning in Hebrew, "the stone of help" (7:12). It is interesting that it was near that site that Israel had been defeated twice before (4:1-2, 5:1). This third battle was really fought in the hearts of the people against that old enemy, Satan. Once Israel achieved victory over their spiritual adversary (7:3-6), the Lord was able to bless their efforts against the Philistines (7:10-14). The term *Amorites* (7:14) is a general name for the original inhabitants of Canaan (cf. Josh. 7:1-7; 10:5; 11:3-5).

The Labors of Samuel (7:15-17)

Samuel the prophet was also a circuit rider judge. He decided legal matters and settled disputes for those on his circuit from Ramah, Samuel's home, after the destruction of Shiloh to Bethel, Gilgal, and Mizpah. In addition to his civil duties as judge and his religious duties as prophet (3:19-20; 7:5-9), Samuel also had military responsibilities in Israel (12:11). Although the following chapters of 1 Samuel continue to record the ministry of this remarkable leader of Israel, the focus is clearly upon a young man named Saul who became Israel's first king.

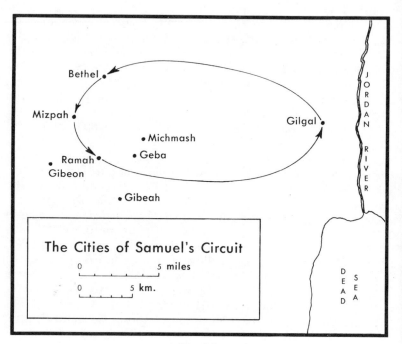

Fig. 1.2

NOTES

1. C. F. Keil and F. Delitzsch, *The Books of Samuel*, trans. James Martin (Edinburgh: T. & T. Clark, 1872), p. 25.
2. William Gesenius, *A Hebrew and English Lexicon to the Old Testament*, ed. Francis Brown, S. R. Driver, and Charles A. Briggs, trans. Edward Robinson (Cambridge: Oxford U., 1959), s.v. "Shemuel."
3. R. Laird Harris, "The Meaning of the Word Sheol as Shown by Parallels in Poetic Texts," *The Evangelical Theological Society Bulletin* 4(1961): 129-135.
4. John J. Davis, *The Birth of a Kingdom* (Winona Lake, Ind.: Brethren Missionary Herald, 1970), p. 34. Neither Samuel nor Christ were of Aaronic descent and thus could not have filled the priestly office.
5. Howard F. Vos, *Archaeology in Bible Lands* (Chicago: Moody, 1977), p. 200.
6. John J. Davis, *Biblical Numerology* (Grand Rapids: Baker, 1968), pp. 87-89.

2

THE REIGN OF SAUL

1 SAMUEL 8-15

ISRAEL'S DEMAND FOR A KING (8:1-22)
  The Demand of the People (8:1-9)
  The Price of Kingship (8:10-18)
  The Decision of the People (8:19-20)
  The Sovereign Permissiveness of Yahweh (8:21-22)

ISRAEL'S ACQUISITION OF A KING (9:1—10:27)
  Saul's Private Anointing (9:1—10:16)
  Saul's Public Presentation (10:17-27)

ISRAEL'S VICTORY OVER THE AMMONITES (11:1-15)
  The Siege of Jabesh-gilead (11:1-5)
  The Destruction of the Ammonite Army (11:6-11)
  The Renewal of the Monarchy (11:12-15)

SAMUEL'S CHARGE TO ISRAEL (12:1-25)
  Samuel's Self-Vindication (12:1-5)
  Samuel's Rehearsal of Israel's History (12:6-12)
  Samuel's Exhortation to Israel (12:13-18)
  Samuel's Words of Assurance (12:19-25)

YAHWEH'S REJECTION OF SAUL (13:1—15:35)
  Saul's Sin at Gilgal (13:1-23)
  Saul's Rash Actions in Battle (14:1-52)
  Saul's Disobedience and Second Rejection (15:1-35)

2

THE REIGN OF SAUL

1 SAMUEL 8-15

The second major section of 1 Samuel brings us to an important milestone in Israel's history—the institution of the monarchy. In response to the pleas of the people, Saul was appointed Israel's first king (1050-1010 B.C.). Saul, a young man from the tribe of Benjamin, was a gifted political and military leader. Although Saul appears to have been a genuine believer (cf. 10:9), his disobedience to the Lord destined his rule for failure and eventuated in his rejection from kingship (15:23). Saul's life illustrates remarkably well the "roller coaster" experience of a carnal Christian. Although Saul functioned as Israel's political and military leader, it was Samuel who continued to serve as the spiritual leader of the nation (12:19-25).

ISRAEL'S DEMAND FOR A KING (8:1-22)

Chapter 8 records Israel's demand for a king—a demand that constituted their rejection of Yahweh as king over Israel (8:7). Although God did not condone their attitude, He permitted the people to follow their own desires and to have a king "like all the nations" (8:5, 20).

The Demand of the People (8:1-9)

The chapter opens with the record of the degeneracy of Samuel's sons, Joel ("Yahweh is God") and Abijah ("Yahweh is my Father"). Those young men were serving as judges in Beersheba, a city situated at the southern extremity of Israel (cf. 3:20), about forty-eight miles south of Jerusalem. Perhaps Samuel, like Eli, was too involved in his ministry to give priority time to his family. God was dishonored as a result. Contrary to God's commands (Deut. 16:18-

20), Samuel's sons perverted justice and used their office and authority for personal gain (8:3).

Three factors contributed to the elders' request that Samuel appoint a king: (1) the corruption of Samuel's sons, (2) the desire to follow the pattern of other nations, and (3) the need for a military commander (8:5, 20). God had made provision in the law for the appointment of a king over His people (Deut. 17:14-15), but the error of the elders was in their failure to recognize God as their true King (8:7; 12:12). From God's perspective, the rejection of His divinely appointed spokesman, Samuel, was in essence a rejection of Him. As Israel had forsaken Yahweh to serve other gods, so they were now turning from Samuel, evidencing their lack of trust in the Lord as their real leader and king. Samuel was displeased with that request but took the matter to the Lord instead of complaining to the people (8:6). God then gave Samuel the responsibility of warning the people concerning the manner of a king—what his rights and prerogatives would be (8:9).

The Price of Kingship (8:10-18)

Samuel warned Israel concerning the price of kingship. He informed the elders of the problems that having a king would bring about. First, a king would draft young men to serve in the military, plow his fields, and prepare for war (8:11-12). Second, a king would draft young women to work in his palace (8:13). Third, a king would tax the people's crops and flocks (8:14-15, 17a). Fourth, a king would appropriate the *best* of their animals and servants (8:16). Finally, a king would place limitations on their personal freedom (8:17b). Samuel also warned the people that they would live to regret their decision and would later cry out for freedom from the rule of the king (8:18).

The Decision of the People (8·19-20)

The elders of the people refused to heed Samuel's warning concerning kingship and reiterated their reasons for requesting a king (8:20). They wanted better justice, military leadership, and to bring their government into conformity with that of other nations. Conformity to the evil ways of unbelievers is always displeasing to the Lord and indicative of spiritual decline (cf. 3 John 11).

The Sovereign Permissiveness of Yahweh (8:21-22)

It was in response to the persistent demand of the people that Yahweh commanded Samuel to appoint them a king (8:22). The response of the Lord to the demands of the people raises some significant questions concerning the will of God.[1] Was it God's will for Israel to have a king? Was it God's will for Israel to acquire a king in the manner in which they were doing it? Was it God's will for Saul to be Israel's king? In answering those questions it is helpful to distinguish three aspects of the will of God. God's *sovereign* will is what God decrees to come to pass. It includes all things (Eph. 1:11) and is irresistible and immutable. God's sovereign will is not fatalism, for God is involved and concerned with man. And man is responsible to God for his actions. God's *preceptive* will is what God prefers or prescribes. This aspect of God's will includes His moral desires as revealed to men in His Word (cf. Exod. 20:1-17). God's *permissive* will refers to what God permits even when it is not in conformity with His revealed or prescribed will. God may permit sin, though it is not in keeping with what He prefers (cf. 1 John 2:1).

Now, back to those three questions. Was it God's will for Israel to have a king? Yes. Prophecies dating back to Moses indicate that it was (cf. Gen. 49:10, Num. 24:17, Deut. 17:14-20). The fact that the monarchy *was* instituted indicates that it was part of God's decree. Well, was it God's will for Israel to acquire a king in the manner in which they were doing it? No. Although it was God's *sovereign* will for Israel to have a king, it was not His *preceptive* will for the nation to acquire a king in the manner in which they were doing it—at the wrong time and with an improper attitude. Nevertheless, God allowed it because it was within His *permissive* will. Finally, was it God's will for Saul to be Israel's king? Of course it was part of the *sovereign* will of God for Saul to be Israel's king; it was part of His eternal decree. But rule by King Saul was apparently not according to God's *preceptive* will for the nation. In the first place, Israel's king was to be from the tribe of Judah (cf. Gen. 49:10), and Saul was of the tribe of Benjamin (9:1-2). Second, Samuel, God's spokesman, warned the people against having a king at that time (8:10-18). Third, the problem was with Israel's timing and attitude. They were rejecting the kingship of Yahweh (8:7) and motivated by a desire to be like the other nations (8:20).

In 1 Samuel 8 it is revealed that God allowed Israel to have a king at that time because it was within His permissive will. That was God's "second best" for the nation. Consequently, He directed Samuel to anoint Saul as king from the tribe of Benjamin (8:22, 9:17). As a result, the people got what they asked for but also received the discipline they deserved (8:18).

How might this truth concerning God's will apply to believers? Well, believers can be sure that they are always in God's sovereign will by His decree (Eph. 1:11). However, like Israel they may forsake God's preceptive will as revealed by His commands. Although believers then may be in God's permissive will, it is not God's best and it may result in divine discipline (cf. Heb. 12:6-11). When believers are in God's sovereign will but out of His preceptive will (i.e., disobedient), then they alone are responsible for their actions. God is sovereign, but man is responsible. With respect to sin and evil, God wills to permit it (cf. Gen. 50:20; Acts 2:23), but not to effect it, for He is not the author of evil (James 1:13).

ISRAEL'S ACQUISITION OF A KING (9:1–10:27)

Chapters 9 and 10 record the appointment of Saul as king over Israel. He was first anointed privately by Samuel and then publically presented to the people of Israel. These chapters illustrate the truth that *all things* are under the control of a sovereign God who directs them to their appointed end.

Saul's Private Anointing (9:1–10:16)

The private anointing of Saul took place while he was searching the hill country for his father's lost donkeys. Verse 1 tells of Saul's family background. His father, Kish, was of the tribe of Benjamin, and like Boaz (Ruth 2:1), was a mighty man of valor. The expression suggests that he was something like a feudal lord—a wealthy land owner and military leader in time of war. His son Saul was a man of stature and impressive physical appearance. He evidenced great potential for leadership and service. The search for the donkeys took Saul north from his home at Gibeah

(10:26), identified with Tell el-Ful about three miles north of Jerusalem, through Shalisha and Shaalim (unidentified) where he then circled back through Benjamite territory to Ramah, the home of Samuel (7:17; 9:18). After his private anointing by Samuel, Saul returned home by way of Gibeath-haelohim, meaning "the hill of God" (10:5, 10). Although the search for the donkeys was unsuccessful, it was providentially used by God to introduce Saul to Samuel who anointed him as king.

Failing in their search for the donkeys, Saul's servant suggested that they search for the well-known prophet Samuel who could possibly disclose the ultimate outcome of their journey. The sovereignty of God is very apparent in vv. 5-14. God was providentially directing the circumstances that brought Saul to Samuel in Ramah. Notice the sequence of events that work together for one purpose: (1) the nation wanted a king, 8:6, (2) Kish lost his donkeys, 9:3, (3) Saul's search was unsuccessful, 9:4, (4) Saul's servant just "happened" to have a gift—an honorarium for the prophet, 9:7-8, and (5) Saul encountered *Samuel* near the gate of the city and asked him for directions to the prophet's house, 9:14, 18. God certainly works *all things* after the counsel of His will—even what appears from human perspective to be loss and failure (Eph. 1:11; Rom. 8:28). What an encouragement to know that God is in control!

The explanatory footnote in verse 9 clarifies for later readers of the books of Samuel that a "seer" (from the Hebrew verb "to see") became known in later times as a "prophet" (from "to prophesy"). There may have once been some distinction between the terms, but not at the time of the writer. Verses 12-14 indicate that Saul met Samuel as he was going to the "high place" to bless a sacrifice and join the people in a feast. A high place (*bamah*) was an elevated place of worship and sacrifice located on a hill or an artificial platform. The custom was essentially Canaanite (cf. Num. 33:52, Deut. 12:2-5), but Israel used such facilities legitimately before the construction of the Temple (cf. 1 Kings 3:2). Unfortunately, the use of such high places eventually contributed to the rise of idolatry among the people of Israel (cf. 1 Kings 11:7, 12:26-33).

God providentially prepared Samuel for his encounter with Saul

by commanding him the day before to be prepared to anoint
Israel's ruler, and then by pointing Saul out, "This one shall rule
over My people" (9:17). It is significant in verse 16 that Saul was
to be appointed as prince (also translated "ruler" or "leader")
rather than king, for the throne belonged to the line of Judah
(Gen. 49:10). When Samuel met Saul he immediately informed
him that his father's donkeys had been found (9:20). Much to
Saul's surprise, he was then invited by Samuel to partake in the
sacrificial banquet that was to be eaten in a hall or room connected
with the high place (9:19, 22). At the banquet Saul was given a
huge portion of the sacrifice, a custom intended to honor him in
the presence of the other guests (cf. Gen. 43:34).

On the day following the feast Samuel privately anointed Saul
as ruler over God's inheritance—Israel (10:1). In biblical times
anointing with oil signified a consecration or setting apart for service. The anointing of a ruler was actually a religious act that
established a special relationship between God and the king who
served as His representative and ruler over His people.[2] Before
sending Saul on his way Samuel promised three signs that would
serve to authenticate Samuel's authority to anoint him ruler over
Israel and thus confirm God's will in the matter (10:2-5, 7). The
three signs would include: (1) an encounter with two men reporting that the donkeys had been found, (2) an encounter with three
men going to Bethel with goats, loaves of bread, and wine, (3) an
encounter with a company of prophets singing prophetic messages
and accompanied by a rhythm band. Verse 5 contains the first
mention in the Old Testament of a "group of prophets." They may
have been members of the "school of the prophets" that some
scholars believe was instituted by Samuel for the purpose of preparing young men for the prophetic ministry (cf. 19:18-20).[3] Saul
was then commanded to wait for Samuel at Gilgal—his first instructions as anointed ruler (10:8).

The signs promised by Samuel were fulfilled to the detail, thus
confirming Saul's appointment (10:9-13). The expression in verse
9, "God changed his heart," literally reads, "God changed him for
another heart." The full meaning of the compact Hebrew phrase
is that "God changed him and gave him another heart." It is debated as to whether that refers to a work of the Spirit of God that

prepared Saul for kingship or the act of regeneration. It most likely refers to both. The record of Saul's life would indicate that he was a regenerate man living a carnal life. Saul was a man who knew God but did not pattern his life after God's will. When the Spirit of God came upon Saul he prophesied mightily (10:10). As a result, the surprised people of Israel circulated an inquiry, "Is Saul also among the prophets?" Some critics view that as an expression of contempt; "What is Saul, a respectable citizen, doing in the presence of these raving prophets?" However, that would reflect a low view of the prophets in the time of Saul that cannot be biblically substantiated (cf. 9:6). The question, "Who is their father?" (10:12) is a response to the proverb and implies that the prophets do not have their prophetic gift by virtue of their birth, but rather by God's sovereign bestowal, and so it was possible for the Lord to give the same gift to Saul.

When Saul returned to Gibeah he related to his uncle the revelation by Samuel that the donkeys had been found. But he said nothing about the anointing or matters relating to the kingdom. By his reference to the "kingdom," the writer masterfully excites the reader's anticipation for what will happen next.

Saul's Public Presentation (10:17-27)

Saul's public presentation to Israel as the nation's divinely chosen ruler took place at Mizpah, the location of the spiritual revival prior to Israel's victorious confrontation with the Philistines (7:5-8). Before the selection of Saul as king, Samuel repeated the substance of his earlier admonition (8:10-18) warning Israel of their independent attitude that involved, in essence, a rejection of God (10:19).

God's choice of Saul to be Israel's king was made apparent through his election by lot (10:20-21).[4] Although the procedure sometimes varied, lot casting was generally a means of determining God's will by asking yes or no questions. One pebble would represent yes and the other no. The lots would be cast like dice into one's lap or a cloth bag. In the Old Testament era lots were cast to select the scapegoat on the Day of Atonement (Lev. 16:7-10), to divide the land after the conquest (Josh. 14:2), and to determine the guilt or innocence of a suspected criminal (Josh.

7:14; Jonah 1:7). The principle underlying the casting of lots is that God is sovereign over human affairs (cf. Prov. 16:33). What appears to be by chance is really a part of God's sovereign design. Lot casting was used prior to the permanent indwelling of the Holy Spirit in believers (cf. Acts 1:26). Since Pentecost, believers are led by the Holy Spirit (Rom. 8:14; Gal. 5:18), and there is no longer any need for lots.

The reference to Saul hiding by the baggage (10:21-23) may reflect his own modesty (cf. 9:21) or perhaps his fear at the prospect of becoming a national leader. Following his selection by lot, Samuel introduced Saul as the one "whom the LORD has chosen" (10:24). That reflects God's sovereignty even in the area of His permissive will. The people of Israel chose to have a king, but God is the one who selected him. Samuel then told the people the ordinances of the kingdom, probably the laws of Deuteronomy 17:14-20 regulating the activities of the king.

After the ceremony at Mizpah Saul returned home to Gibeah (Tell el-Ful), located just three miles north of Jerusalem on the main road to Shechem. Gibeah served as the first capital of the Israelite monarchy. As Israel's first king, Saul had active supporters (10:26) but political enemies as well (10:27). Certain worthless men questioned his leadership and refused to honor him in the customary way. But Saul wisely held his peace in order not to provoke the situation.

ISRAEL'S VICTORY OVER THE AMMONITES (11:1-15)

Chapter 11 is intended to show how the initial opposition against Saul was overcome as the new king proved himself worthy of Israel's allegiance. The military campaign against the Ammonites served to unite Israel (11:7), organize the military (11:8, 11), and bring about Saul's acceptance as king (11:14-15).

The Siege of Jabesh-gilead (11:1-5)

Shortly after Saul's public appointment to kingship (10:17-27), it was learned that the Israelite city of Jabesh-gilead was under siege by Nahash (whose name means "serpent"), commander of the Ammonites. The city of Jabesh-gilead either gave its name to or received its name from the Wadi Yabis (Jabesh) that flows into the Jordan from the east about twenty-five miles south of the Sea of Galilee. Although the exact location of Jabesh-gilead is debated (either Tell el-Maqlub or the dual sites of Tell Meqbereh and Tell Abu Kharaz)[5] the city was within a night's walk of Beth-shan to the northwest (cf. 31:11-13). The Ammonites were descendants of Lot (Gen. 19:38) and occupied Transjordan desert fringes east of the territories of Gad and Manasseh.

The terms of surrender demanded by Nahash included thrusting out the right eye of the inhabitants of the city (11:2). Not only would that be a great humiliation to the people of Jabesh-gilead, but it would also disable their warriors, for the left eye was generally behind a soldier's shield in battle. The elders of Jabesh asked for a seven-day delay before surrender hoping for deliverance by the Israelites west of the Jordan. Nahash agreed to the proposal, apparently because he was not prepared to take the city by force and did not expect any help to come to the inhabitants of Jabesh-gilead.

When the report came to Saul at Gibeah he was working as a farmer plowing a field (11:5). Evidently he did not seize the reins of government at once but continued his work as a farmer while he waited for a time when he could answer Israel's expectations of him as a king and deliver the nation from its enemies (cf. 8:6, 20).

The Destruction of the Ammonite Army (11:6-11)

As the Spirit had come upon Gideon and Samson (Judg. 6:34; 14:6), so the Spirit of Yahweh came upon Saul in a mighty way, empowering him to deliver the desperate citizens of Jabesh-gilead. Saul's anger and quick response to the request may reflect the fact that he owed his very existence to Jabesh-gilead. Back in the period of the judges during the Benjamite War (Judges 20-21) the Israelites had sworn, "None of us shall give his daughter to Benjamin in marriage" (Judg. 21:1, 7, 18). Later, in order to provide wives for the men surviving the conflict, four hundred young virgins were captured from Jabesh-gilead. It is quite probable that Saul had descended from one of those marriages. Naturally "his anger burned exceedingly" when he heard that Jabesh-gilead was threatened. To call the tribes to arms Saul slaughtered his oxen and sent the pieces throughout Israel with the message, "Whoever does not come out after Saul and after Samuel, so shall it be done to his oxen" (11:7). For a similar rather shocking "call to arms," note Judges 19:27—20:1.

All the Israelite tribes responded to Saul's call to arms, and 330,000 warriors assembled at Bezek (Khirbet Ibziq), a city located seventeen miles north of Shechem. The distinction made between Israel and Judah (11:8; 15:4; 17:52), indicates that the book was written after the division of the kingdom (931 B.C.). A message of encouragement and promise of deliverance was immediately communicated to the people of Jabesh-gilead.

Saul followed a surprise tactic, dividing his forces into three companies and then attacking the Ammonites at the "morning watch." The morning watch was the last of three night watches— the first from 9:00-12:00 P.M., the second from 12:00-3:00 A.M., and the third from 3:00-6:00 A.M. (cf. Lam. 2:19; Judg. 7:19; Exod. 14:24-27). The early morning attack probably took place about dawn before the Ammonites had girded on their armor for battle. Jabesh-gilead was delivered, and the Ammonites were scattered and soundly defeated.

The Renewal of the Monarchy (11:12-15)

As a result of his victory over the Ammonites Saul gained the support and allegiance of the people of Israel as their king. Although some advocated the executions of those who had previously questioned his rule (11:12; cf. 10:27), Saul recognized that God had accomplished the deliverance for Israel and refused to heed the suggestion of his overly zealous supporters. Samuel then invited the people to Gilgal, the first Israelite camp west of the Jordan at the time of the conquest (cf. Josh. 4:19). The site is probably to be identified with Khirbet el-Mefjer about a mile northeast of Old Testament Jericho. The ceremonies at Gilgal involved a confirmation of the kingdom in the hand of Saul and an affirmation of the people's commitment to their new king.

SAMUEL'S CHARGE TO ISRAEL (12:1-25)

Chapter 12 records Samuel's farewell address at Gilgal in which he defended his judicial administration and relinquished the leadership of the twelve tribes to Saul. Samuel did, however, continue his priestly and prophetic functions in Israel (cf. 12:23; 13:8-12; 15:30-31; 16:13).

Samuel's Self-vindication (12:1-5)

Although Hannah had promised that her son would be devoted to lifelong Levitical service (1:11), Samuel recognized the wisdom of stepping aside from the sphere of political leadership to encourage the Israelites to look to Saul as the leader of the nation. Samuel began his charge to Israel seeking to establish his own integrity. Confident of his moral record, Samuel invited any accusation of injustice, making obvious reference in verse 3 to his sons' failures (cf. 8:3, 5). The Israelites responded by declaring Samuel's innocence of any injustice or bribery (12:4-5).

Samuel's Rehearsal of Israel's History (12:6-12)

Samuel then proceeded to rehearse the history of God's "righteous acts" toward Israel (12:7). That history lesson begins with the Exodus and concludes with Israel's demand for a king. Twice before in Israel's history—during the Egyptian bondage and the Canaanite oppression—the people had cried out to God for deliverance. Yet after the divine deliverance came, they soon forgot the Lord and returned to their evil ways (12:9, 12). Israel's demand for a king was another evidence of their continuing unfaithfulness to the Lord.

The otherwise unknown judge, Bedan, mentioned in verse 11 probably represents a scribal error in transmission. How would a reference to an unknown judge serve to advance the argument? The name recorded in the Septuagint and Syriac versions is "Barak," Deborah's general (Judg. 4:6-16). However, it is more likely that the original text read *Abdon* (cf. Judg. 12:13-15). The first letter (*'ayin*) apparently dropped out of the Hebrew name '-B-D-N and was later vocalized by the Masoretes as "Bedan."[6]

Samuel's Exhortation to Israel (12:13-18)

Although God gave Israel a king in accordance with the demands of the people, Samuel warned Israel that the king would procure the anticipated deliverance only if they would fear the Lord and give up their rebellion against God. The "fear of the

Lord" (12:14) is the theme of the Israelite wisdom literature
(Prov. 1:7; Psalm 111:10). The fear of the Lord is set in parallel
construction with departing from evil (Job 28:28) and obeying
His commandments (Eccles. 12:13), phrases that well define how
the fear of the Lord is applied in one's life. Although the consequences of obedience are not stated in 1 Sam. 12:14, blessing is
implied by the contrast in verse 15.

Lest any should doubt his word, Samuel called upon the Lord
to authenticate his message to the people by sending rain and
thunder (12:17). In Palestine, the rainy season is in the winter.
In March the rainfall begins to taper off with the "latter rain"
(Deut. 11:14, KJV), so necessary for a good harvest, coming in
April and early May. Rain during the wheat harvest (late May
and early June) would be unusual indeed.

Samuel's Words of Assurance (12:19-25)

Samuel's farewell to Israel concluded with two great promises.
Having exhorted the people to faithfully serve the Lord, Samuel
promised that Yahweh will never forsake His people (12:22).
That promise is based upon God's own "name." In the biblical
period a name represented a person's character and reputation.
Israel was assured that God will never abandon them because it
would be inconsistent with His reputation for faithfulness (cf.
Exod. 34:6; Deut. 31:6; Josh. 1:5; Heb. 13:5).

The second promise was given by Samuel in response to the request of the people (12:19, 23). Samuel assured Israel that he
would not sin against God by ceasing to pray for them. The life of
Samuel illustrates the truth that prayer is an essential ingredient
to an effective ministry (7:5; 8:6; 1 Thess. 5:17; James 5:16).
Samuel's farewell discourse closes with a formula for blessing
(12:24-25; cf. Deut. 30:15-20). The people are reminded that the
fall of the monarchy and exile of the nation would be the ultimate
divine judgment on disobedience (cf. Deut. 28:41, 63-64).

YAHWEH'S REJECTION OF SAUL (13:1—15:35)

Chapters 13-15 record two of Saul's most important campaigns—
one directed against the Philistines to the west and the other

against the Amalekites to the south. It was in those campaigns that Saul demonstrated by his self-sufficiency and carnality that he was unfit to be king over Israel and as a result was set aside by God as Israel's king (13:14; 15:26).

Saul's Sin at Gilgal (13:1-23)

One reason the people of Israel wanted a king was to lead them in battle against their enemies (8:20). In Saul's day the greatest threat to the security of the Israelites in Palestine was the Philistine menace. Those powerful military people had established military outposts in the hill country as part of their strategy to subjugate Israel. Apparently Saul did not plan for a major attack on the Philistines immediately, but mobilized three thousand troops to secure the capital, Gibeah, and the region just to the north. Verse 1 appears to be a chronological note recording the date of the first battle with the Philistines in relationship to the beginning of Saul's reign. It reads literally, "Saul was one year old when he became king and ruled two years over Israel." Although the age of Saul at his accession is nowhere else recorded, Acts 13:21 states clearly that he ruled Israel forty years. Verses 1-2 may best be understood, "Saul was one and _____ (perhaps forty) years old when he began to reign, and when he had reigned two years over Israel then Saul chose for himself three thousand men of Israel. . . ."

While Saul was in Michmash, identified with modern Mukhmas just seven miles north of Jerusalem, Jonathan struck the Philistine garrison at Geba, identified with Jeba', one and a half miles southwest of Michmash across a deep ravine. The news of the victory sounded forth to all Israel via the ram's horn (literally, "shofar"). The Philistine responded to that initial defeat by assembling a great force of chariots at Michmash while Saul called the people to Gilgal to ask God's favor before engaging in battle (13:4).

The number of Philistine chariots is much too large (cf. Exod. 14:7; Judg. 4:13; 2 Chron. 14:9), and probably represents a scribal error. The steep terrain of the hill country would render such a large number of war chariots quite useless. It is best to follow the Lucian edition of the Septuagint and the Syriac that reads three thousand. The mighty response of the Philistines to the attack on

Geba wrought fear in the hearts of the Israelites and some even retreated across the Jordan (13:6-7).

Verse 8 presents a rather difficult chronological problem. Just after his anointing, Saul had been commanded by Samuel to go to Gilgal and wait there for him seven days in anticipation of Samuel's sacrifice (10:8). The reference in 13:8 is obviously to the same event. Although some would attempt to compress the events of 10:8–13:14 into seven days, and liberal critics would say that 10:8 is misplaced, it is better to understand the record as indicating that Saul waited for Samuel in Gilgal according to the agreement that had been made two years earlier (cf. 13:1-2).[7] It had apparently been agreed after his anointing that Samuel would meet Saul at Gilgal for sacrifice and worship prior to any major engagement with the Philistines. But rather than waiting for Samuel as he had been instructed, Saul offered the burnt offering *himself* in order to unify the people and prepare them for war (13:9).

Perhaps Samuel's delay was intended as a test of Saul's obedience. When Samuel arrived at Gilgal just after Saul finished the sacrifice, the disobedient king sought to justify himself instead of confessing his sin (13:11). Samuel soundly rebuked Saul for his disobedience and appeal to "situation ethics" and declared that his reign would not be perpetuated by being passed on to his descendants. The Lord would seek another king who would be more sensitive to His will (13:13-14). When Samuel returned to Gibeah, Saul found himself with a mere six hundred men to defend the hill country. As a result, the Philistine reinforcements were able to carry out punitive expeditions against Israel to the north, west, and south (13:17-18).

Verses 19-23 record the fact that the Philistines had a monopoly on iron and metal-working craftsmen early in the monarchy. That situation, which continued until the time of David (1 Chron. 22:3), accounts in large measure for the military superiority of the Philistines. Although the Philistines were able to make iron implements, the peoples of the surrounding nations had to make due with weapons of bronze.

Saul's Rash Actions in Battle (14:1-52)

While Saul was relaxing on the outskirts of his capital, Gibeah,

Jonathan made plans to attack a Philistine stronghold near Mich-mash. The "ephod," a priestly garment (Exod. 28:8-14; 1 Sam. 2:28; 14:3), was used in the Old Testament era to consult God (cf. 23:9-12). That was probably done by means of the Urim and Thummim that were attached to the breastpiece (cf. Exod. 28:15-30). Like lot casting, the ephod enabled the priests to determine God's will when faced with two alternative courses of action. Verses 4-5 describe the geographical setting for the assault (see figure 2.1). Even today one can stand at Michmash (Mukhmas) and look down toward the deep wadi that Jonathan and his armor bearer crossed. Jonathan expressed his faith in verse 6 by declaring to his armor bearer that "the LORD is not restrained to save by many or by few." He recognized that the Lord is never limited by the lack of His people's abilities, powers, or resources.

Jonathan's assault was not a foolhardy risk but is seen in verses 9-10 to be directed by the Lord. It was agreed that the Philistines' shout that the two could come up to them would serve as a sign from the Lord. The invitation given by the enemy (v. 12) was in fact a sign by which the Lord proclaimed His will. The two war-riors were then able to climb up the steep ravine undetected and overcome the twenty or so Philistines occupying the outpost (14:14).

When Saul's spies observed the confusion in the Philistine camp due to Jonathan's raid, Saul called for the priest to determine God's will. The statement in verse 18 concerning the Ark appears to con-tradict the words of 7:2 that indicate the Ark was at Kiriath-jearim at the time. Although it may have been brought to Gibeah tempo-rarily, it may be better to follow the Septuagint that reads "ephod," an object used in determining God's will (cf. 14:3). After calling for the ephod (or Ark) Saul told the priest to cancel the inquiry; he did not have time to consult God (14:19)! Hearing the report of the initial victory, the "Hebrews who were with the Philistines" (either deserters or mercenaries) returned, and those who had avoided the initial confrontation joined in battle (14:21-22). By means of divine intervention (cf. 14:15, 23) the Israelites were able to achieve a decisive victory over the Philistines. The name *Beth-aven* ("house of evil") is probably a purposeful perversion of

the name *Bethel* ("house of God") reflecting the writer's condemnation of the idolatry that was instituted there by Jeroboam I (1
Kings 12:26-33; Hos. 10:5).

Verse 24 records Saul's foolish order that none of his soldiers
should eat until he avenged himself against the Philistines. So de-
sirous of avenging himself, Saul neglected the needs of his men.
His foolish oath weakened the fighting potential of Israel and almost cost him the life of his son. Due to his absence Jonathan did
not hear his father's oath and helped himself to some honey during
the pursuit of the Philistines (14:27). Utterly exhausted by their
eighteen-mile pursuit of the enemy from Michmash to Aijalon
(identified with Yalu, east of traditional Emmaus), the Israelite
warriors began to eat captured Philistine livestock without first
draining the blood. That was in direct violation of Leviticus
17:10-14—"You are not to eat the blood of any flesh." Realizing
the seriousness of the offense, Saul rebuked the people and proceeded to sacrifice the animals, being careful to drain the blood.

Saul was anxious to finish off the Philistines, but he decided to
ask God's counsel in the matter (14:36-37). He had previously
neglected to inquire of the Lord (14:19), and now God was silent—
an evidence of the further estrangement between Saul and the
Lord. God's silence led Saul to believe there was sin in the camp,
and so he initiated an investigation announcing the death penalty
for the offender. Note the irony of verse 39. That was Saul's second foolish oath (cf. 14:24). Beware of making foolish promises
that are impossible to keep. By casting lots it was determined that
Jonathan was the one in violation of Saul's foolish oath. Although
Saul was ready to put his own son to death, the people of Israel
defended their hero, and Jonathan's life was spared (14:44-45).

Verses 47-52 contain a summary of Saul's military achievements.
Saul expanded his kingdom to the south (Edom), east (Ammon
and Moab), north (Zobah), and west (Philistia). The defeat of
the Amalekites is recorded in chapter 15. Saul's foreign policy was
to defend Israel by attacking and defeating nations that could
threaten Israel's security. Although not an imperialist, Saul was an
aggressively minded defender of the young nation at a crucial time
in Israel's history.

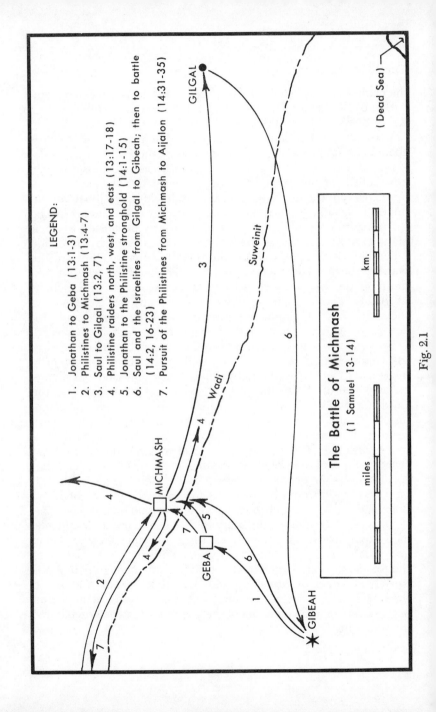

LEGEND:

1. Jonathan to Geba (13:1-3)
2. Philistines to Michmash (13:4-7)
3. Saul to Gilgal (13:2, 7)
4. Philistine raiders north, west, and east (13:17-18)
5. Jonathan to the Philistine stronghold (14:1-15)
6. Saul and the Israelites from Gilgal to Gibeah; then to battle (14:2, 16-23)
7. Pursuit of the Philistines from Michmash to Aijalon (14:31-35)

The Battle of Michmash
(1 Samuel 13-14)

miles

km.

Fig. 2.1

Saul's Disobedience and Second Rejection (15:1-35)

In chapter 15 the Amalekite war is recounted in detail because it led to the final breach between Saul and Samuel and resulted in Saul's rejection by God as king. The Amalekites, nomadic descendants of Esau (Gen. 36:12), were ancient foes of Israel. They fought against the Israelites at Rephidim (Exod. 17:8-13) and were placed under divine judgment by the Lord (Deut. 25:19). Through Samuel, God's spokesman, Saul was commanded to strike the Amalekites and put them under the ban (*herem*). That involved devoting the city, persons, animals, and possessions to the Lord for destruction in accordance with Deut. 7:2-6; 12:2-3; 20:16-18. Although that may seem severe, the command came from a perfectly just God and was the just execution of judgment on sin (cf. 15:2, 18). Although the Amalekites were soundly defeated, the Kenites were spared (15:4-6). The Kenites were nomadic Midianites (Num. 10:29; Judg. 1:16) who were well disposed toward Israel from ancient times (Exod. 2:18; 18:9-10). The campaign against the Amalekites proceeded from Havilah in northwest Arabia, east toward Shur, that is near the eastern border of Egypt.

By sparing Agag, the king of the Amalekites, and keeping the best of the spoil, Saul violated the ban and disobeyed the direct word of God (15:8-9). When confronted by Samuel at Gilgal, Saul first lied (v. 13) and then excused himself by blaming the people (v. 15). Verse 11 is not an indication of changeableness in God's essential nature or plans (cf. 15:29; James 1:17), but rather records God's grief and sorrow at the sinful rebellion of Saul (cf. Gen. 6:6).

When Samuel rebuked Saul for his flagrant disobedience to God's command, Saul again affirmed his innocence and blamed the people for taking the spoil for "sacrificial" purposes (15:20-21). Samuel, of course, saw through Saul's explanation and pointed out God's priority of obedience over sacrifice. Sincere obedience is the prerequisite for pleasing service for God. All conscious disobedience is essentially an act of idolatry because it elevates self above God. Rejection of God's word resulted in Saul's being rejected as king over Israel (15:23, 26).

In response to Samuel's rebuke, Saul confessed that he feared the people and listened to them instead of God. Although he had confessed his sin Samuel thought it wise to separate himself from Saul since God had rejected him from being king. As Samuel turned to go, Saul grabbed his robe and tore it—a vivid picture of the fact that God had torn the kingdom from Saul (15:27-28). The "Glory (literally, Eminence) of Israel" is a unique designation for God emphasizing His eternal nature, a concept very appropriate in the context of His immutability (15:29; cf. Num. 23:19).

Saul was concerned that he not appear to have lost Samuel's support, and Samuel graciously consented to go with him to worship the Lord. Samuel may have discerned that Saul's confession in verse 30 was more sincere than that recorded in verse 24. True confession and repentance is the result of genuine sorrow for offending God, not just because of a fear of judgment and disgrace.

Agag, whom Saul had spared, was put to death by Samuel (15:32-33). The fact that Agag was hewn to pieces "before Yahweh" indicates that the execution was in fulfillment of the ban and was in fact the judgment of God. Just how Agag came to Samuel is a difficult problem in translation, for the Hebrew text is unclear.[8] It may be that he came "trembling" or "hesitant" saying either, (1) "Surely the bitterness of death is past," or (2) "Now comes bitter death."

Both Samuel and the Lord were grieved over the disobedience that had disqualified Saul from the kingship. Although he remained the man in power, he was no longer the man of choice (13:14; 15:28). Verse 35 indicates that Samuel did not "see" Saul again for the rest of his life. However, 19:24 records that Saul was with Samuel at Ramah. The solution to the apparent discrepancy is that the Hebrew verb to see can mean "to give attention; take heed; or regard with interest." The point is that as God was through with Saul as king, so was Samuel. Saul was qualified to be a great leader in Israel, but his independent spirit and lack of obedience destroyed his potential for serving the Lord and his country.

First Samuel 15 is very significant in preparing the way for David's accession to the throne. That has been demonstrated by Herbert Wolf's studies of the Hittite "Apology of Hattusilis"—a thirteenth-century dynastic defense.[9] In that document a king or his supporters outline the reasons why his rule is legitimate. That kind of defense would be particularly necessary in the case of kings who founded new dynasties and could be charged with usurping the throne. That was the case with both David and Hattusilis, who founded new dynasties. In the dynastic defense the disqualification of the preceding ruler is described in detail. Saul's disqualification from the kingship is certainly the major thrust of chapter 15. The similarity between the "Apology of Hattusilis" and 1 Samuel 15 is remarkable. That literary form could help to explain the purpose and arrangement of the biblical narrative. In the context of 1 Samuel the main point of chapter 15 is that in light of Saul's disqualification from the kingship, David's anointing and rise to power is not to be questioned or subject to criticism.

NOTES

1. J. Barton Payne, "Saul and the Changing Will of God," *Bibliotheca Sacra* 129 (October-December 1972): 321-25.
2. Roland De Vaux, *The Bible and the Ancient Near East* (Garden City, N.Y.: Doubleday, 1967), pp. 152-66.
3. Hobart E. Freeman, *An Introduction to the Old Testament Prophets* (Chicago: Moody, 1968), pp. 28-34.
4. John Lindblom, "Lot-casting in the Old Testament," *Vetus Testamentum* 12 (1962): 164-78.
5. Elmer B. Smick, *Archaeology of the Jordan Valley* (Grand Rapids: Baker, 1973), p. 85.
6. Gleason L. Archer, Jr., *A Survey of Old Testament Introduction* (Chicago: Moody, 1964), p. 273.
7. For a thorough discussion, see John P. Lange, *Commentary on the Holy Scriptures: Samuel*, ed. Philip Schaff (Grand Rapids: Zondervan, n.d.), pp. 11-13.
8. Robert G. Bratcher, "How Did Agag Meet Samuel? (1 Sam. 15:32)," *The Bible Translator* 22 (October 1971): 167-68.
9. Herbert M. Wolf, "Implications of Form Criticism for Old Testament Studies," *Bibliotheca Sacra* 127 (October 1970): 299-307.

3

THE RISE OF DAVID

1 SAMUEL 15-31

David's Rise as Shepherd (16:1—17:58)
David's Selection and Private Anointing (16:1-13)
David's Entrance into Royal Service (16:14-23)
David's Encounter with Goliath (17:1-58)

David's Service in Saul's Court (18:1—20:42)
The Covenant of Friendship (18:1-5)
The Development of Saul's Jealousy (18:6-9)
The Results of Saul's Jealousy (18:10—19:10)
The Escape of David from Saul's Court (19:11-24)
The Intervention of Jonathan for David (20:1-42)

David's Adventures as a Fugitive (21:1—31:13)
David's Flight to Nob (21:1-9)
David's Flight to Gath (21:10-15)
David's Flight to Moab (22:1-5)
Saul's Destruction of the Priests of Nob (22:6-23)
David's Rescue of the City of Keilah (23:1-14)
Jonathan's Encouragement of David in the Wilderness (23:15-18)
Saul's Pursuit of David in the Wilderness of Maon (23:19-29)
Saul's Life Spared in the Wilderness of Engedi (24:1-22)
Samuel's Death (25:1)
David's Marriages (25:2-44)
Saul's Life Spared Again (26:1-25)
David's Return to Philistia (27:1-12)
Saul and the Witch of En-dor (28:1-25)
David's Rejection by the Philistines (29:1-11)
David's Rescue of the Inhabitants of Ziklag (30:1-31)
Saul's Death on Mount Gilboa (31:1-13)

3

THE RISE OF DAVID

1 SAMUEL 15-31

David, the great grandson of Ruth and Boaz, was the youngest son of his father, Jesse. His youthful years of shepherding sheep in the hills near Bethlehem were providentially used by God to prepare King David to shepherd Israel. David is known in Scripture as a man after God's own heart (13:14) and was "hand-picked" by God to rule His people (1 Kings 8:16). So exemplary was his faith among his people that the God of Israel was called the God of David (2 Kings 20:5; Isa. 38:5). David contributed greatly to the worship of Yahweh in Israel both in planning the building of the Temple (2 Chron. 1:4) and in writing psalms for praise and worship (2 Sam. 23:1). The historical setting of many of the seventy-three Davidic psalms may be found in the books of Samuel.

David's life was far from perfect, and the Bible does not gloss over his sins and failures. David's life illustrates the truth that no believer is immune to the enticements of sin, and even sincere confession and repentance cannot deliver a sinner from the inevitable and devastating consequences of sin. Even believers will reap what they sow (Gal. 6:7).

The life of David, Israel's first king from the tribe of Judah, may be divided into three major periods: David's rise to power (1 Sam. 16-31), David's triumphs (2 Sam. 1-10), and David's troubles (2 Sam. 11-20). The rest of 1 Samuel records David's preparation for the office of king with special emphasis on the relationship between David and King Saul.

DAVID'S RISE AS SHEPHERD (16:1–17:58)

Chapters 16-17 record David's private anointing and reveal how

David's musical and military abilities brought him to King Saul's own side.

David's Selection and Private Anointing (16:1-13)

While Samuel was still mourning over Saul's disobedience and failure (cf. 15:22-23), God instructed him to anoint a new king from among the sons of Jesse. Samuel's fear of Saul (16:2) is connected with the geographical situation. To go to Bethlehem (located about five miles south of Jerusalem) from Ramah, Samuel would have to pass through Gibeah, Saul's capital. Samuel's concern was not unwarranted in light of Saul's spiritual degeneracy and violent temper (cf. 18:11). The Lord did not suggest that Samuel deceive Saul in the matter, but told the prophet to perform the anointing in Bethlehem while officiating at a sacrifice to avoid arousing the suspicions of Saul.

The visit of Samuel at Bethlehem was unexpected, and the town elders apparently assumed that he had come to pronounce and execute judgment (cf. 7:15-16, 15:33). Having assured them that he had come in peace, Samuel commanded the elders that they consecrate themselves in preparation for the sacrifice (16:5). To *consecrate* literally means "to set apart" for special purposes. That was done by means of ceremonial washings and purifications (cf. Exod. 19:10, 14, 22). Note that Jesse and his sons were also consecrated and invited to the sacrifice. The stage was set for David's anointing.

Although Samuel was certain that David's older brother Eliab must be God's appointed king, the Lord instructed him that from a divine perspective a man's heart is of greater importance than his physical appearance. It was only after Jesse's seven sons passed before Samuel that David, the shepherd boy, was brought to the sacrifice. The Lord then revealed to Samuel that David was the king of His choosing (16:12). The phrase *in the midst of* (verse 13) may be translated "from the midst of." Like Saul's first anointing (9:26–10:1), it is probable that David's first anointing was a private matter. This was the first of three anointings for David. The second was his anointing as king of Judah (2 Sam. 2:4), and his third was as king over all Israel (2 Sam. 5:3). The descent of the Spirit of Yahweh upon David would empower him to fulfill the specific tasks God had appointed him to accomplish.

The meaning of the name *David* has been the subject of considerable discussion. The discovery of the word *dawidum* in the Mari texts as a title meaning "commander" or "chieftain" has led some to conclude that *David* was a title of office, and the original name of Jesse's youngest son was *Elhanan* (cf. 2 Sam. 21:19). However, that view has been soundly refuted in a paper delivered at the Old Testament Congress in Oxford in 1959.[1] It is probable that the name *David* means "beloved one" or perhaps "uncle" (cf. Amos 6:10).

David's Entrance into Royal Service (16:14-23)

Verse 14 records that after the anointing of David, the Spirit of Yahweh departed from Saul. The chaotic situation during the rest of Saul's rule reflects the fact that the Spirit was no longer empowering Saul to serve as king. It is important to remember that whereas the indwelling of the Holy Spirit in the Old Testament era was selective and temporary, in the church age it is universal among believers and permanent (cf. 1 Cor. 12:13, Rom. 8:9). The "evil spirit from Yahweh" has been understood in various ways: (1) demonic possession as divine punishment, (2) demonic attack or influence, (3) an evil messenger like the one sent to entice Ahab (1 Kings 22:20-23), or (4) a spirit of discontent created by God in the heart of Saul (cf. Judg. 9:23). Since Saul appears to have been a believer (cf. 10:6, 9), it is quite unlikely that he would have been demon-possessed. The contrast with the Spirit of Yahweh would rule out a "spirit of discontent" view. The verse should probably be understood to mean that God sovereignly appointed a demon, one of Satan's emissaries (cf. Matt. 12:24), to torment Saul. That may have been intended by God to drive Saul to his knees so that he might look to the Lord for help. The verse points to the fact that God is *sovereign* over all spiritual powers—even Satan and his assistants. Apparently God allowed Saul's consequent fits of insanity and rage (cf. 16:15; 18:11; 19:10; 20:33) to demonstrate his rejection rather than immediately dismissing him from the office of king.

Whatever Saul's malady was, it was temporarily relieved by music. The royal court searched the land for a skillful player of the lyre, an instrument similar to, but smaller than, the harp. David was selected to stand before the king and refresh Saul's spirit with his instrumental selections (16:23). Other significant qualities and abilities that led to David's appointment are recorded in verse 18. David's appointment as Saul's armor bearer probably took place after he killed Goliath (cf. 17:55-58) but is mentioned here because it fits well with the theme of David's entrance into royal service. It was clearly part of God's plan to have David, the shepherd boy, learn about court life and the kingdom firsthand.

David's Encounter with Goliath (17:1-58)

In chapter 17 David's ability to lead and rule Israel is demonstrated by his victory over the Philistine giant, Goliath. In the record of that encounter the testimony of David's faith and demonstration of his military ability serve to confirm his anointing.

Verse 15 indicates that David divided his time between serving Saul in the royal court (apparently when Saul's sickness necessitated it) and tending his father's flocks in Bethlehem. It was during an absence from the royal court that the Philistine and Israelite armies gathered for battle in the Elah valley, about fifteen miles west of Bethlehem. The Philistines were camped between Azekah (Tell Zakariyeh) and Socoh (Khirbet Shuweikeh) on a hill south of the valley. The specific site, Ephes-dammim ("boundary of bloodshed"), has not been identified. Saul and the warriors of Israel were situated on the hill to the north of the valley.

The Elah valley would have been well adapted for the movement of the Philistine chariots had it not been for a deep ravine with steep banks in the middle of the valley that made it quite difficult to cross. The defensible positions of the two armies and the danger involved in advancing through the deep ravine help to explain the delay before engaging in battle (cf. 17:16). Anxious to begin warfare, the Philistine giant, Goliath, suggested a contest between champions in behalf of the armies (17:8-10). In ancient times, battles were often decided by a contest between selected warriors (cf. 2 Sam. 2:12-17). The problem facing the Israelites was that of finding a challenger for Goliath.

Goliath, from the Philistine city of Gath (Tell es-Safi), was "six cubits and a span" tall. Since a cubit is approximately eighteen inches, and a "span" is nine inches, it can be calculated that Goliath stood nine feet, nine inches tall. His coat of armor weighed five thousand shekels or approximately 125 pounds. The head on Goliath's bronze spear weighed approximately seventeen pounds—considerably more than the standard shot put. Goliath may have been a descendant of the gigantic sons of Anak (cf. Josh. 11:22) who had struck fear in the hearts of the Israelites before the conquest (Deut. 9:2). Perhaps Saul and his warriors had forgotten the victory God gave Israel in the conquest, for they too were dismayed and greatly afraid of this formidable foe.

While David was tending his father's sheep near Bethlehem, his three older brothers were down the Elah valley with Saul and the warriors of Israel. At Jesse's request David journeyed down the Elah valley to the battlefield in order to carry provisions to his brothers and return with a report concerning his brothers' welfare (17:17-18). Upon arriving at the camp David heard the shouting of the warriors and rushed to the battle line just in time to hear Goliath's challenge and witness the trembling of the warriors of Israel (17:23-24). David was quickly informed that King Saul had promised riches, freedom from taxes and public service (cf. 8:11-17), and his daughter's hand in marriage to the one who could defeat Goliath (17:25). That promise was confirmed to David as he questioned other warriors.

Refusing to be daunted by his oldest brother's rebuke (17:26, 28-30), David let it be known to King Saul that he would fight the Philistine giant (17:32). David recounted his past victories over the lion and the bear and declared his faith in God's power to deliver him from the hand of Goliath (17:34-37). Refusing Saul's heavy armor and weapons, David confronted the giant with a shepherd's sling and five smooth stones from the brook that flows down the Elah valley during the rainy season (17:37-40).

Goliath's pride was offended when he saw that the Israelites had sent a young shepherd boy into the battlefield as his challenger. In response to his cursing, David warned the giant of his impending doom and then declared the *theological* purpose of his mission. Although Goliath came to do battle with full armor and several weapons, David came in the name of Yahweh, commander of the armies of heaven ("hosts") and the armies of Israel (17:45). Since one's name stands for the person and his reputation, David was saying that his dependence would not be upon weapons of war, but upon the well-known strength of the Lord (cf. Exod. 15:3). David intended his victory over Goliath to teach the Philistines—indeed, "all the earth"—that (1) the God of Israel exists, and (2) that Yahweh delivers His own in spite of the military superiority of the enemy (17:46-47). With one well-placed stone from his sling David struck the Philistine warrior on his unprotected forehead and then decapitated him with the giant's own sword (17:48-51).

When the Philistines saw that their champion was dead, they fled for home while the Israelites pursued them north toward Ekron and east toward Gath. David took Goliath's head to "Jerusalem" (17:54)—apparently a reference to the Israelite portion of the city (Josh. 15:63; Judg. 1:8) outside the Jebusite fortress that was not taken until David became king over all Israel (2 Sam. 5:6-9). The giant's weapons were kept by David for a time at his own home (*tent* means "dwelling place," as in 4:10; 13:2) but were later deposited in the priests' sanctuary at Nob (21:9).

After witnessing David's accomplishments in the battlefield Saul inquired concerning his father (17:55). Saul knew David as his court musician (16:18-23), but had apparently forgotten the name of David's father and needed to know it in order to reward David's family for the victory (cf. 17:25, "his *father's* house").

DAVID'S SERVICE IN SAUL'S COURT (18:1—20:42)

Chapters 18-20 describe David's service in Saul's court. The story is told in terms of the relationship between David and Jonathan. It is the author's purpose to show that the very man David displaced in succession to the throne was his best friend, and that Saul's own son acknowledged the legitimacy of David's rule.

The Covenant of Friendship (18:1-5)

It was after the slaying of Goliath that David went to live with Saul in the royal palace at Gibeah. Although David continued to serve as court musician (18:10), he also functioned as Saul's armor bearer when Israel went out to do battle (cf. 16:21). The friendship between David and Saul's son, Jonathan, blossomed quickly. Verse 1 records that the soul of Jonathan was literally "knotted" to the soul of David. It was a relationship characterized by loyalty, love, personal devotion, and self-sacrifice (cf. Lev. 19:18; John 13:34-35).

The covenant of friendship referred to in verse 3 was a unilateral (binding on one party only) covenant in which Jonathan committed himself to David with complete disregard for self. The gifts given by Jonathan served to ratify the covenant and honor David. As David proved himself faithful as court musician and armor bearer, he was soon elevated to a prominent position of leadership in the military (18:5).

The Development of Saul's Jealousy (18:6-9)

The enduring relationship between David and Jonathan is set in stark contrast to the relationship between David and Saul, which soured because of the king's jealousy. David's success as a warrior was immortalized in the lyrics of a popular folk song of the era, "Saul has slain his thousands, and David his ten thousands" (18:7). The increasing popularity of David brought fear and suspicion to the heart of Saul (18:9, 12, 15, 29). Here was David, a young man with unique abilities and obvious divine blessing, coming into the limelight rather quickly. Saul did not like it. He soon became jealous. Saul's jealousy of David not only destroyed their relationship, but also ate away at Saul like a cancer and was a significant factor in his own decline. Verse 8 contains a note of irony. To Saul it appeared that there was nothing left for David to obtain but the *kingdom*. That was no mere conjecture, but rather a foregone truth.

The Results of Saul's Jealousy (18:10–19:10)

As David's reputation began to outweigh Saul's, the king's jealousy increased and began to manifest itself. That jealousy has a destructive effect on relationships is clearly seen here. To Saul, David came to represent an enemy. Saul's attempt to pin David to the wall with his spear is the first illustration of the destructive effects of jealousy (18:10-12). That happened twice before Saul had David removed from his position as "minister of music" and had given him a commission in the military. Saul was apparently hoping that David, a young and inexperienced officer, would be killed leading his men in battle (cf. 18:17). On the contrary, David continued to prosper as he engaged in military activity ("went out and came in before them"), gaining the love and respect of all Israel (18:14-16).

Not only did Saul threaten David's life; he refused to fulfill his promise to give David his daughter in marriage. Although Saul had promised his daughter to the one who killed Goliath (17:25), he later conditioned the reward on further conquests, hoping that David would not live to collect "the prize" (18:17-18). Saul then furthered the dishonesty by giving his oldest daughter, Merab, to another man (18:19).

Saul had hoped that David would lose his life fighting the Philistines in order to win the hand of Merab. When that plan failed, Saul was delighted to learn that his younger daughter, Michal, loved David (18:20). He decided to use the offer of Michal's hand as a means of leading David to his death. Although David did not have sufficient funds for a "dowry" (the "bride price" or payment to the father as compensation for the loss of a daughter), Saul suggested a creative alternative. Instead of the traditional dowry, David was asked to present Saul with the foreskins of one hundred Philistines (18:25). Since no Philistine would willingly submit to circumcision, the foreskins would serve as tangible proof that one hundred Philistines had been slain. David exceeded Saul's requirement by bringing the foreskins of two hundred Philistines, and won the hand of Michal in marriage (18:27). His success in killing the Philistines was convincing evidence to Saul that Yahweh was with David.

Having failed in his previous attempts to lead David to his death, Saul told his son Jonathan and all his servants to take the necessary steps to assassinate David (19:1). Jonathan's friendship revealed itself in action as he warned David of Saul's murderous intentions and then intervened in David's behalf (19:3-5). Saul was persuaded by Jonathan's words and pronounced an oath not to put David to death. Translated literally, Saul said, "As Yahweh lives, if I put David to death . . . ." The consequence of violating the oath is too terrible for Saul to speak (19:6). Jonathan even

convinced Saul to restore David to his former position as "minister
of music" in the royal court. But David's military successes again
aroused Saul's animosity and he made a *third* attempt to pin David
to the wall with his spear (19:8-10).

The Escape of David From Saul's Court (19:11-24)

The rest of chapter 19 records how David's life was spared by
the deception of Saul's daughter Michal. It is ironic to find two
of Saul's children, Jonathan and Michal, seeking to preserve the
man who is destined to take Saul's throne. Having been warned by
Michal of a plot on his life, David escaped Jerusalem and fled
to Samuel at Ramah (19:18-19). Naioth was apparently a community in Ramah where the school of the prophets was situated
(cf. 19:19-20). Michal delayed the discovery of David's escape
by telling Saul's messengers that David was sick. The household
idol (*teraphim*, Gen. 31:19, 30-35) was used to deceive the messengers into believing that David was in bed. Since such household idols were usually quite small, it may be that the idol was not
in bed, but *near* the bed. That is suggested by the basic meaning
of the Hebrew preposition used in verse 13. It may have been
customary to keep such an idol near a sick person. The quilt and
clothes could have been used to make it appear as though David
was home sick in bed.

Michal resorted to situation ethics in order to save David. But
God's Word declares that lies and deception are never justified,
no matter how noble the purpose (cf. Exod. 20:16; Prov. 24:28).
Sad to say, the presence of a household idol, usually kept in a
small shrine in the home, also reflects some compromise in David's
faith. That example would later have devastating consequences
for his son Solomon (cf. 1 Kings 11:1-8).

When David's assassins showed up in Ramah, their evil plans
were thwarted by the Spirit of God. Saul's messengers all prophesied by the Spirit of God and apparently joined the school of the
prophets (19:20-21). When Saul himself decided to go to Ramah
and capture David, the Spirit of God came upon him in an unusual
way. Saul stripped himself of his outer garments and prophesied
before Samuel all day and night. Perhaps the Spirit of God was at

work in Saul's heart during that time, seeking to bring him to repentance.

The Intervention of Jonathan for David (20:1-42)

Chapter 20 records how David's loyal friend, Jonathan, made one final attempt to intervene in David's behalf and have him restored to Saul's graces. While Saul was being detained by the Spirit of God at Ramah, David made his way to Gibeah to confer with Jonathan concerning the matter of the king's threats on his life. Although Jonathan expressed his certainty that Saul was not seeking David's life (20:2-3), he may have been unaware of the events of 19:8-24 and was trusting in his father's solemn oath not to harm David (19:6). David then devised a plan to determine Saul's attitude toward him—for good or evil (20:4-7). The new moon (20:5) was celebrated with a sacrificial meal (cf. 2 Kings 4: 23; Isa. 1:13; Amos 8:5) and served both as a religious and civil festival (Num. 10:10; 28:11-15). David's family apparently got together for an annual family reunion that coincided with one of those monthly celebrations (20:6, 28-29).

It was within the context of making plans for determining Saul's attitude toward David that Jonathan openly acknowledged that Yahweh would eventually destroy David's enemies. The implication was that one day Saul would be judged by God, and David would be Israel's new king. With that in mind, Jonathan requested protection for his family when David took the throne (20:14-15). After devising plans for secretly informing David whether he would be safe in Saul's court or should flee (20:18-23), David hid in a field to await the outcome of Jonathan's efforts.

During the first night of the feast Saul did not question David's absence, assuming that he was ritually unclean and thus could not participate in the meal (cf. Lev. 7:20-21; 15:16). It was not until the second day that Saul questioned Jonathan about David's failure to attend the feast. When Jonathan gave the explanation (20:27-29), Saul expressed his anger in very offensive language (20:30). As Jonathan tried to defend David's integrity, the king made an attempt on the life of his own son (20:33). To Jonathan, the message was clear. Saul had decided to put David to death.

Jonathan knew that David was no longer safe in the court of

Saul and would have to flee. The secret sign for David's departure was given by Jonathan as he shot the arrows into the field (20:22, 37). In the parting of the two friends, their covenant bond is again stressed (20:41-42). The two men wept before they parted. Although both were valiant warriors, they were men of tender hearts. From that point until Saul's death, David was a fugitive from Saul and an outcast from the royal court.

DAVID'S ADVENTURES AS A FUGITIVE (21:1–31:13)

David now entered a long period of separation from the royal court. Most of that time was spent fleeing from Saul, who saw David as his number one enemy. Through David's adventures as a fugitive he learned lessons on prayer, trusting the Lord, and how to praise God. That is evidenced by many of the Davidic psalms that have their background in chapters 21-31 (cf. Psalms 18; 34; 52; 54; 56; 57; 63; 124; 138; 142).

David's Flight to Nob (21:1-9)

After his farewell to Jonathan, David journeyed south from Gibeah to Nob, a community of priests situated on Mount Scopus, about a mile north of Jerusalem. Somewhere along the way David arranged a rendezvous with a small band of men (21:4-5; cf. 22:2). There at Nob, David deceived Ahimelech the priest into thinking that he was on official business for the king (21:2). David's lying and deception later precipitated a tragedy for the priests of Nob (22:9-18). David made two requests of Ahimelech. He first asked for bread (21:3). Ahimelech informed David that the only bread on hand was the "consecrated bread," the showbread that was set apart for use in the Tabernacle and was to be eaten only by the priests (Exod. 25:30; Lev. 24:5-9). After inquiring as to whether David's band of men were ceremonially clean (cf. Lev. 15:16), Ahimelech gave David the showbread. He apparently recognized that his *moral* obligation to preserve David's life superceded the *ceremonial* regulation concerning who could eat the consecrated bread. Jesus referred to that incident in Matthew 12:3-4 and Mark 2:25-26 in His discussion concerning the Sabbath with the Pharisees. Jesus pointed out that service to God may supercede the ceremonial Sabbath law. Both Ahimelech and Jesus recognized that whereas

God's moral law is inviolable, ceremonial regulations can be super-seded by moral obligations and service to God. That is consider-ably different from situation ethics, which holds that God's moral law (that which reflects His character) can be disobeyed, depend-ing upon the circumstances.

David's second request of Ahimelech was for a weapon (21:8-9). He was given the sword of Goliath, the Philistine giant he had killed in the Elah valley (cf. Chapter 17). The narrator records in verse 7 that David's visit with the priests of Nob did not go unde-tected. Doeg, an Edomite shepherd of Saul, witnessed the encoun-ter and passed the word along to the king (cf. 22:9-10). Doeg is re-ferred to as "chief" among Saul's herdsmen. The term is literally translated "strong one" and suggests his rather violent nature, which would be evidenced later (cf. 22:18-19). Just why Doeg was "de-tained before Yahweh" at Nob is a matter of speculation. Perhaps he was there to fulfill a vow, undergo ritual cleansing, or be in-spected for leprosy (cf. Lev. 13:4).

David's Flight to Gath (21:10-15)

Since David's life was endangered as long as he remained in Saul's realm, he fled southeast to Philistine territory. With a subtle appreciation for humor, the writer records that David went right to Gath, Goliath's hometown, wearing the giant's old sword. Per-haps he had intended to enlist as an unknown soldier in the service of Achish, but David's plans were foiled as he was immediately recognized. David is referred to in verse 11 as "king of the land." Although his anointing would not have been known to the Philis-tines, his well-known exploits commended him as king of Israel.

When David realized that he had been recognized by the Philis-tines, he feared for his life and feigned insanity to persuade Achish to send him away. That incident in the life of David provides the background for Psalms 34 and 56. David's performance before Achish enabled him to escape but marks a low point in his career. Note that in Psalm 34 Achish is referred to as Abimelech ("father of a king"). That was probably not a name, but a dynastic title frequently used by the Philistines (cf. Gen. 20:2; 26:1).

David's Flight to Moab (22:1-5)

The first part of chapter 22 records how David took his parents across the Dead Sea to Moab, the homeland of his great grandmother Ruth, to protect them from the evil intentions of Saul. After David's escape from Gath he began to organize his affairs by gathering his followers and family together at a cave near the strategic city of Adullam (Tell esh-Sheikh Madhkur) about ten miles southeast of Gath. There in a cave not far from the Philistine border David composed Psalm 57 and possibly Psalm 142. Before long David had become the captain of four hundred men—an army that was soon to grow to six hundred (cf. 23:13).

Out of concern for his parents' safety and well-being David took them across the Dead Sea to Moab where they would be out of Saul's reach. Mizpeh ("watchtower") was probably a fortress in Moab. Some have suggested that it be identified with Kir (modern Kerak), the ancient capital of Moab. David's family ties with Moab are recorded in Ruth 1:4-18 and 4:21-22. Returning from Moab, David spent some time at the "stronghold." Transliterated "Mesudah," this may refer to Masada, the mountain fortress towering 1,320 feet above the shores of the Dead Sea (cf. Psalms 18:2; 62:2). Following the advice of the prophet Gad, David left the fortress and hid out in a forest located a few miles southeast of Adullam.

Saul's Destruction of the Priests of Nob (22:6-23)

The rest of chapter 22 illustrates Saul's apostasy and David's priestly support. Saul's slaughter of innocent priests and their families is a further evidence of his spiraling degradation and departure from the Lord. Sitting under a tamarisk tree with spear in hand, Saul began to complain to his servants. In verse 7 a negative response is anticipated. Saul is suggesting that the Benjamites could not expect blessings under the rule of David of the tribe of Judah. Saul's complaint in verse 8 is threefold. In essence Saul accused his son of disloyalty, his subjects of apathy, and David of conspiracy.

Doeg, who had observed David's visit at Nob, then sought to ingratiate himself to King Saul by reporting how Ahimelech had given David provisions and a weapon (22:9-10). Ahimelech and the priests of Nob were then summoned before Saul and accused of conspiracy against the throne. In defending himself Ahimelech inadvertently defended David. He argues that David is one who turns aside to your bodyguard (22:14). There is evidence in Exodus 3:3 and Ruth 4:1 that "turn aside" may mean "have access to." Apparently Ahimelech's argument was that David had free access among those who protected Saul's life. How could he be considered an enemy? Ahimelech declared that he was innocent by reason of his ignorance of matters relating to this affair (22:15).

Although Saul condemned Ahimelech and the priests to death, his servants knew better than to raise their weapons against the priests of Yahweh. Doeg, however, saw this as a further opportunity to gain Saul's favor and carried out the slaughter of eighty-five priests, men, women, infants, and animals (22:16-20). Only Abiathar escaped to report the tragedy to David. Although that bloodbath constituted a partial fulfillment of the prophesied judgment on Eli's house (2:27-36), Saul was ultimately responsible for that condemnable act. The sovereignty of God never cancels out the responsibility of man (cf. Acts 2:23).

When Abiathar reported the tragedy, David realized the devastating consequences of his lie to Ahimelech (cf. 21:1-2). Full of regret, David recognized how his own sin had precipitated in the slaughter of the priests of Nob (22:22). David offered Abiathar protection from Saul, and Abiathar remained with David, giving him valued priestly support. As priest, Abiathar carried the ephod with which David could inquire of the Lord (cf. 23:2, 6, 9).

David's Rescue of the City of Keilah (23:1-14)

First Samuel 23:1-14 shows how David served Israel even during the days of his exile from the royal court. Keilah (Khirbet Qila), a city of Judah about three miles south of Adullam, was being plundered by the nearby Philistines who would raid the threshing floors after the Israelites had harvested and processed the grain. David first sought the Lord's will concerning the matter and then went and delivered the inhabitants of Keilah (23:2-5). One might wonder why David inquired of the Lord *twice*. Perhaps it was because his men were fearful and needed the assurance that victory would come through God's help (cf. 23:3-4).

It was while David was still at Keilah defending the Israelite city that Saul made plans to capture him within the city walls (23:7-8). Saul mistakenly assumed that since he had the opportunity to capture David, it must be God's will. Believers ought not be deceived into thinking that an open door of opportunity is a clear indicator of God's will. Verse 6 does not mean that only after the deliverance of Keilah did Abiathar flee to David (cf. 22:20-23), but that Abiathar accompanied David to Keilah and was there to assist the Lord's anointed in determining God's will. Although David had delivered Keilah, many of its inhabitants remained loyal to Saul. In light of that situation David had two questions for God: (1) Would Saul come to Keilah in pursuit of David? and (2) Would the people of Keilah betray David to Saul (23:11-12)? Receiving a yes answer to both questions, David and his six hundred men escaped to the wilderness.

The wilderness of Judah is the desolate, barren area between the hill country and the Dead Sea. Many ravines and caves are found in that rugged region. As David used the wilderness as a place of refuge from Saul, so did the Jewish zealots seeking refuge from Rome during the first (A.D. 66-73) and second (A.D. 132-35) Jewish revolts. The wilderness of Ziph is the wilderness surrounding Ziph (Tell Zif), just four miles southeast of Hebron.

Jonathan's Encouragement of David in the Wilderness (23:15-18)

These verses record the last meeting between David and his loyal friend Jonathan. There in the wilderness at Horesh ("forest") Jonathan sought out and encouraged David, assuring him that he would be the next king over Israel (23:17). Jonathan exemplifies the attitude of servanthood Paul encourages in Philippians 2:3-11. Although he knew his position as Saul's heir to the throne, Jonathan was content to take second place to God's anointed king, David. Before parting, the two friends renewed the covenant that had been made earlier (18:3; 20:12-17). In Proverbs Solomon says, "There is a friend who sticks closer than a brother" (18:24). Jonathan was that kind of friend.

Saul's Pursuit of David in the Wilderness of Maon (23:19-29)

The last part of chapter 23 records David's narrow escape from king Saul in the wilderness of Maon. That was the most dangerous situation David had yet encountered and provides the historical background for Psalm 54. After Jonathan's visit with David in the wilderness the Ziphites came to Saul at Gibeah, reporting precisely where David was hiding out (23:19). The people of Ziph promised to betray David into Saul's hand. Knowing that David was proficient at eluding his pursuers, Saul commissioned the Ziphites to reconnoiter the situation and report back to him afterward. Verse 23 reflects the fact that David was well acquainted with the hiding places in the wilderness. He had learned the geography of that area as a shepherd during his youth.

Apparently after spying out the situation the Ziphites led Saul into the wilderness of Maon in pursuit of David. Several geographical terms appear in verse 24. The "wilderness of Moan" was the barren territory in the vicinity of the city of Maon, about five miles south of Ziph. The Arabah (meaning "wasteland") generally refers to the Rift Valley north and south of the Dead Sea. However, in this context it refers to a desert area in the wilderness of Judea. Jeshimon means in Hebrew "desert or waste" and refers to the wilderness southeast of Hebron (26:1-3). In the wilderness of Maon Saul and his men surrounded David (23:26). But in the providence of God a messenger came to Saul reporting a Philistine raid in the north. Saul had to return home, thus allowing David to escape. The site was named the "Rock of Escape" to commemorate the deliverance provided by the Lord (23:28). Verse 29 appears as the first verse of chapter 24 in the Hebrew text.

Saul's Life Spared in the Wilderness of Engedi (24:1-22)

Chapter 24 records how Saul's life was spared by David because of his respect for the sanctity of the throne. The point of the chapter is that while David founded a new dynasty, he was not an usurper who took the life of the preceding king. After Saul had responded to the Philistine raid (23:27), he led three thousand warriors in search of David in the wilderness of Engedi. Engedi (meaning "spring of the kid") was an oasis east of Hebron situated

above the shores of the Dead Sea. The area in the immediate
vicinity of that freshwater spring, noted for its lush vineyards
(Song of Sol. 1:14), stands in stark contrast with the surrounding
desert. The limestone that dominates that region is permeated
with caves, providing good hiding places for a fugitive like David.

In the sovereignty of God, Saul entered the very cave where
David was hiding (24:3). The Hebrew expression used in verse 3,
"to cover his feet" (KJV), is a euphemism for having a bowel
movement. Although David refused the suggestion of his men to
kill the king, he was able to cut off a piece of Saul's robe unde-
tected. David's conscience later troubled him on account of that,
for touching Saul's clothing was tantamount to touching his person, and David knew it was wrong to raise his hand against the
Lord's anointed king (24:6, 10).

When Saul left the cave David called out after him and bowed
down before him. He honored Saul as Yahweh's anointed king
over Israel even though Saul was his personal enemy. David
pointed out to Saul that although he had been given the opportunity to take the king's life, he had refused to do so (24:10-11).
Rather than taking matters into his own hand, David trusted the
Lord to bring about justice (24:12, 15; cf. Deut. 32:35; Rom.
12:17-21). In verse 14 David likens himself to a dead dog and a
single flea. The point of the verse is that David was perfectly
harmless to Saul.

Upon hearing David's testimony of non-aggression, Saul was
moved with emotion and acknowledged that David was more
righteous than himself. Although David had done him well, Saul
had treated David wickedly (24:17-19). Although Saul's remorse
appears to be sincere, it was only temporary (cf. 26:1-6). Verse
20 is really the climax of the chapter, for there Saul acknowledges
that David will inevitably become king (cf. 23:17). In light of
that acknowledgement Saul made two requests (24:21). He asked
David to (1) preserve his family, and (2) preserve his family
name. David agreed to those requests and kept his promise (cf.
2 Sam. 9, 21:6-8). While Saul returned home to Gibeah, David
remained in hiding (24:22). He was apparently unconvinced by
Saul's expressions of remorse.

Samuel's Death (25:1)

The death of Samuel, the last of the judges and first of the prophets, brought Israel to the end of an era. Samuel's death is probably recorded here because it took place around the time that David was at Engedi. So universal was Samuel's popularity among the people that all Israel gathered to lament his death. Samuel was buried at his house in Ramah, perhaps in a garden burial chamber as in the case of Manasseh (2 Kings 21:18; 2 Chron. 33:20). Verse 1 also records that David went down to the wilderness of Paran, a desert area in the northeast region of the Sinai Peninsula. The Septuagint reads "wilderness of Maon." Although "Maon" may be the correct reading in 25:1, it is possible that it reflects assimilation with "Maon" in 25:2.

David's Marriages (25:2-44)

The rest of chapter 25 records David's encounter with Nabal and describes how David came to marry Abigail in addition to his wives Michal and Ahinoam. While hiding out in the wilderness David and his men took a job protecting the flocks of a prosperous businessman named Nabal. Although his place of business was in Carmel (Kermel), seven miles south of Hebron, his home was actually in Maon (Khirbet Main), a mile farther south. Nabal's name means "fool," and his manner of conducting himself indicates that the name is appropriate (25:25). Abigail, his wife, was a woman of intelligence, beauty, and humility (25:3). After protecting the flocks and possessions of Nabal for some time (25:15-16, 21), payday finally arrived, and David sent ten of his men to collect their rightful due. David sent his men to collect their wages on a "festive" (literally, "good") day—a day of prosperity and celebration due to the income received from the sale of newly sheared wool (25:2, 8, 36).

When David's servants came to collect their wages (25:5-9), Nabal not only refused to remunerate David and his men for their services, but he pretended not to know David or anything about their agreement (25:10-11). David determined to collect by force that which was owed him and took four hundred of his men to confront Nabal (25:12-13).

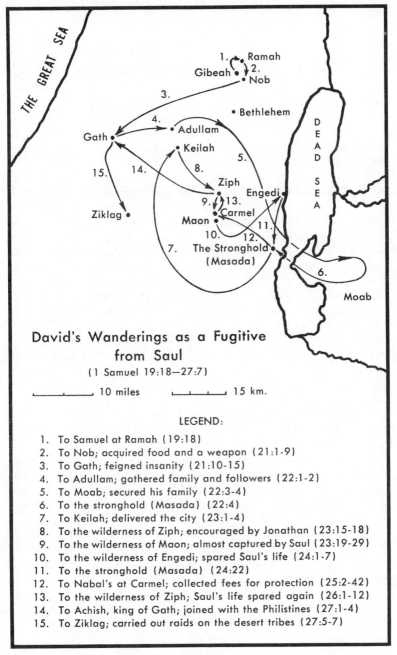

David's Wanderings as a Fugitive from Saul

(1 Samuel 19:18—27:7)

⊢────────┐ 10 miles ⊢──┴──┴──┐ 15 km.

LEGEND:

1. To Samuel at Ramah (19:18)
2. To Nob; acquired food and a weapon (21:1-9)
3. To Gath; feigned insanity (21:10-15)
4. To Adullam; gathered family and followers (22:1-2)
5. To Moab; secured his family (22:3-4)
6. To the stronghold (Masada) (22:4)
7. To Keilah; delivered the city (23:1-4)
8. To the wilderness of Ziph; encouraged by Jonathan (23:15-18)
9. To the wilderness of Maon; almost captured by Saul (23:19-29)
10. To the wilderness of Engedi; spared Saul's life (24:1-7)
11. To the stronghold (Masada) (24:22)
12. To Nabal's at Carmel; collected fees for protection (25:2-42)
13. To the wilderness of Ziph; Saul's life spared again (26:1-12)
14. To Achish, king of Gath; joined with the Philistines (27:1-4)
15. To Ziklag; carried out raids on the desert tribes (27:5-7)

Fig. 3.1

While David and his men were on their way to deal with Nabal, it was reported to Abigail that her husband had scorned David and deprived him of his rightful due (25:14-17). Recognizing the futility of debating the matter with her foolish husband, Abigail gathered sufficient goods together to compensate David for his services. She sent those provisions before her as she started down the mountain to meet David (25:18-19).

When Abigail suddenly met David face to face on the road, she quickly dismounted from her donkey and prostrated herself before David. Her address to David is a masterpiece reflecting feminine charm, wisdom, and grace (25:24-31). In that potentially disastrous situation, Abigail intervened by (1) confessing the wrong done David, (2) making restitution to David, (3) asking forgiveness for the transgression, and (4) recognizing David's right to the throne. She wisely points out to David that needless shedding of blood would not be within his own best interests at that time (25:21-22, 31). The phrase in verse 29, "bound in the bundle of the living," is a metaphor that reflects the custom of binding valuables in a bundle to protect them from injury. The point of that verse is that God cares for His own as a man would his valuable treasure. David was quick to acknowledge the wisdom of Abigail's words. He accepted her provisions and promised her peace (25:32-35).

While Abigail was taking care of her husband's business obligations, Nabal was home getting drunk (25:36). Intoxicated, Nabal apparently suffered a stroke and became paralyzed. That is reflected in verse 37 which records that "his heart died within him so that he became as a stone." Ten days later Nabal died—the fatal blow of God's divine judgment on his life. That incident in the life of David well illustrates how God executes judgment and avenges His own (cf. Deut. 32:35; Rom. 12:19).

The chapter concludes by recording how David offered Abigail, Nabal's widow, a marriage proposal. She accepted and became his wife (25:39-42). David later had a son, Chileab, by Abigail as recorded in 2 Samuel 3:3. Two of David's other wives are referred to in verses 43-44. That marks the beginning of David's royal harem in violation of Deut. 17:17 (cf. 2 Sam. 3:2-5). By noting that Michal was given by Saul to another man, the narrator reminds the readers that David was still living under Saul's threat. That is further evidenced in the next chapter.

Saul's Life Spared Again (26:1-25)

Chapter 26 records how Saul's life was again spared by David. The incidents related here are similar to those in chapter 24, but the differences are sufficient to establish the fact that there are two different adventures recorded. While David was hiding out in the wilderness of Ziph, the Ziphites informed Saul for a second time as to the place of David's hiding (23:19; 26:1). Again Saul led three thousand of his men into the wilderness in pursuit of David. However, it was Saul who was taken by surprise rather than David. As Saul and his soldiers were sleeping at night, David and his nephew Abishai (cf. 1 Chron. 2:15-16) stole into the king's camp. Saul was quickly spotted at the center of the camp with his spear—Saul's symbol of authority (cf. 18:10; 19:9)—stuck into the ground at his head. Abishai wanted to take advantage of the opportunity to slay Saul, but David again refused to lift up his hand against the Lord's anointed (26:9). David was not an usurper. He would not assassinate Israel's anointed king. David knew that God would remove Saul from office by His own means and according to His own perfect timing (26:10). Instead of taking Saul's life, David took his spear and water jug to be used as proof that he had been close enough to Saul to kill him. David's visit to Saul's camp, explains the narrator, went undetected because the Lord had caused a "deep sleep" (KJV) to fall upon the people (26:12). That expression is used in Gen. 2:21 of the "deep sleep" that fell upon Adam while God fashioned Eve.

After crossing a valley to a distant hill David shouted back a taunt to Abner, who was in charge of guarding the king (26:14-16). He held up Saul's spear and water jug as evidences of Abner's negligence and David's own good will. Although he clearly had an opportunity to kill Saul, he had refused to do so. David had three questions for Saul, who was awakened by the shouting (26:18). In essence, David demanded an explanation for Saul's continual hostility toward him. David expressed his willingness to offer an atoning sacrifice to God if there has been any offense on his part (verse 19). On the other hand, if evil men had caused Saul's hostility toward David, they should be judged. The phrase, "Go, serve other gods," reflects David's feeling that his exile from the land was virtually equivalent to forcing him to abandon the worship of Yahweh, for there were no sanctuaries to Yahweh outside Israelite territory.

As in 24:17, Saul confessed his sin and wrongdoing. In addition, he invited David to return, promising not to make another attempt on his life. Although Saul may have been sincere, he could not be trusted, and David wisely did not accept that invitation. After offering the return of Saul's spear, David requested that his life be valued as much as he valued Saul's (26:24). As the two parted Saul recognized the certain success of David's future as Israel's king (26:25; cf. 24:20). That was the last meeting of King Saul and David, the king-elect.

David's Return to Philistia (27:1-12)

Placing little confidence in Saul's promise to do him no harm (26:21), David again sought refuge outside of Israelite territory. As he had done earlier when fleeing from Saul, David went to Achish, king of Gath (21:10-15). The sixteen months he spent in Philistine territory (27:7) prepared David for later Philistine wars by giving him the opportunity to become familiar with the geography of Philistia. When David returned to Gath, he was welcomed by Achish who had no doubt by this time heard of the split between Saul and David. Perhaps Achish was anxious to strengthen his army with David's six hundred fighting men. After living for some time in Gath, twelve miles east of Ashdod, David requested a city of his own in the country. It has been suggested that David wanted to be free from the constant surveillance to which he would be exposed in Gath and that he wanted to avoid the pagan influence of a Philistine city.[2] Achish established David as a Philistine vassal, giving him the city of Ziklag (Tell esh-Sheriyeh), located about thirteen miles northwest of Beersheba.

David used Ziklag as a base for his raids on the northern Sinai desert tribes. Among those were the Amalekites, well known as Israel's enemy (cf. 15:2-3). David was actually attacking the enemies of Israel while he pretended to serve the interests of Achish (27:8-10). David left no survivors from those raids in order that Achish might not learn the true nature of his desert exploits. The term *Negev* (meaning "dry land" or "south country") refers to the geographical region south of the hill country, centering around Beersheba. David's deception was so effective that Achish was convinced that he would serve him forever. In actuality, David was beginning his conquest of the surrounding nations—a task he would complete as king (cf. 2 Sam. 8).

Saul and the Witch of En-dor (28:1-25)

Chapter 28 marks the spiritual low point in Saul's life and records one of the darkest hours of his reign as king. With the Philistines ready to attack Israel, Saul resorted to spiritism, only to learn of his own impending death and Israel's defeat. In his preoccupation with his pursuit of David, Saul apparently neglected the growing Philistine threat to Israel. The Philistines, resorting to a new strategy, marched into the Jezreel Valley where they could use their chariots, thus cutting off Saul from the northern tribes. David, at this time, was not only in the Philistine army, but had been appointed the bodyguard for King Achish (28:1-2). Verse 2 records David's response to Achish regarding his participation in the war with Israel. The words of David were ambiguous and not a definite commitment to go to war against Israel. Had David refused to participate, he could not have escaped death; he was forced to wait for divine deliverance from that predicament. As the plot thickens, the reader is reminded that Samuel is dead. No encouraging word from the Lord would be forthcoming (28:3). Verse 3 also notes that Saul had removed mediums and those delving in the realm of spirits from the land (cf. Deut. 18:9-13; Exod. 22:18; Lev. 19:31). That provides the background for the incident that follows.

The Philistines were camped at Shunem (modern Solem), a city in the valley of Jezreel situated on the south slope of the Hill of Moreh. The Israelite forces were camped five miles to the south at Mount Gilboa (28:4, cf. 31:1). Saul was so afraid as he faced this battle that his heart "trembled greatly" (28:5). The same word is used in Exodus 19:18 of the *quaking* of Mount Sinai at the giving of the law. Saul inquired of the Lord, but the heavens were silent. God did not respond by dreams as He had to Joseph, or by

the Urim and Thummim as He had to the high priest (see com-
ments on 14:3), or by prophetic revelation as He had with Samuel (28:6). The comment of the chronicler (1 Chron. 10:14) is
not a contradiction, but points to the fact that Saul went to the
medium for counsel rather than *persistently* seeking a word from
the Lord. That was not a harsh or unjust act on God's part, for
Saul had been given many opportunities to repent and discover
God's will, but he had refused to do so (cf. 19:23-24).

With the heavens silent, Saul sought out a medium to enable
him to determine the outcome of the battle with the Philistines.
Saul was informed by his servants that at En-dor, between Mount
Tabor and the Hill of Moreh, there lived a medium who had escaped his purge (28:3, 7). In the Hebrew, the phrase translated
medium literally reads, "a woman who is a mistress of necromancy," that is, one who consults the dead to determine the future. The Old Testament law forbade necromancy (divination by
means of communion with the dead) and called for the death
penalty on any who would consult mediums (Lev. 19:31; 20:6,
27; Deut. 18:10-11). Saul disguised himself and traveled under
the cover of darkness to En-dor to consult the medium. Assuring
her that she would not be punished for practicing her forbidden
profession (Exod. 22:18), he requested that she bring up Samuel
from the dead (28:11).

The medium carried out Saul's instructions, but rather than
using the tricks of her trade to deceive Saul, she was very much
surprised to see an old man appear whom Saul identified as Samuel (28:14). That appearance of Samuel has been interpreted in
various ways by scholars and theologians. Some have suggested
that the appearance of Samuel was *psychological*—in the mind of
Saul. Two arguments against that view are that (1) the woman
also saw Samuel, v. 12; and (2) Saul actually talked with Samuel,
v. 15. The church Fathers held the view that a *demon imperson-
ated Samuel* and appeared to Saul. But the message recorded in
28:16-19 would have hardly come from a demon. Still others have
concluded that the medium was a *fraud* and *tricked* Saul into
thinking that he saw Samuel. Yet, the medium was surprised by
Samuel's appearance (28:12) and that would not have been the
case had it been planned.

It seems best to follow the view of the rabbis that verses 12-19 record a genuine appearance of Samuel that God Himself brought about. There are at least five arguments in favor of this interpretation. First, the medium was surprised, indicating that something happened that she was not expecting (28:12). Second, Saul identified the figure as Samuel and bowed down in respect for the prophet. It is unlikely that Saul, who knew Samuel so well, would have been deceived by an impersonation. Third, the message Samuel spoke was clearly from God (28:16-19). Fourth, the biblical text itself says that the figure was Samuel (28:12, 15, 16). It is clear that the author, under divine inspiration, intended the readers to understand that Samuel actually appeared to Saul. Fifth, a similar appearance of men from the dead took place when Moses and Elijah appeared at Christ's transfiguration (Matt. 17:3). There is nothing inherently difficult with God bringing about a posthumous appearance of Samuel the prophet.

Confronted with Samuel, Saul explained his dilemma and requested the prophet's counsel. The Philistines were attacking Israel. What should he do? Samuel proceeded to remind Saul that the kingdom had been taken from him because of his disobedience in the Amalekite war (28:17-18). He then predicted Israel's defeat and the deaths of Saul and his sons at the hands of the Philistines (28:19). Samuel never really answered Saul's question, "What should I do?" In essence the prophet was saying, "Saul, there is nothing that can be done. Because of your disobedience, your fate is sealed."

Saul was terrified because of the message of doom that Samuel had communicated to him (28:21). The future was clear. Judgment was imminent and certain. All that had been Saul's as king would soon be lost because of his rebellion and contempt for God's will. Having received some nourishment, Saul departed with his servants to return to the camp of Israel at Mount Gilboa.

David's Rejection by the Philistines (29:1-11)

Chapter 29 records how God delivered David from the distressing situation of having to join with the Philistines in a war against his own fellow Israelites. Chronologically, chapter 29 preceeds chapter 28, for 28:4 records that the Philistines *were* camped at Shunem in the Jezreel Valley, whereas 29:1, 11 indicates that they gathered at Aphek and then *went up* to Jezreel. The incidents of chapter 28 are recorded first because they provide the spiritual background for Israel's defeat and Saul's death. The proper order of events is as follows: Saul gathered his army at a spring in Jezreel near the foot of Mount Gilboa, while the Philistines rallied at Aphek in the Sharon plain. From there the Philistines advanced along the Via Maris to Shunem at the foot of the Hill of Moreh, while Saul deployed his army opposite them on the lower slopes of Mount Gilboa. From there Saul went to the medium at En-dor, and the next day met his death in battle.[3]

With the Philistines preparing to fight Israel, what should David do? If he refused to fight, he risked being killed by the Philistines for treason. Yet if he fought Israel, how could he later be honored as Israel's king? David had no choice but to wait and trust the Lord to provide a means of escape from the predicament. The Lord's solution to that situation was to stir up mistrust of David in the hearts of the Philistine warriors (29:2-4). The "lords of the Philistines" (rulers of the Philistine cities, 6:16) demanded that David and his men be sent back to Ziklag for fear that they might turn on the Philistines in the heat of battle. What better way to appease Saul ("his word") than to return to his service with the heads of the Philistine warriors (29:4).

Quite apologetically, Achish dismissed David from serving in the Philistine militia and was released to return to Ziklag (24:6-10). In response to his dismissal David—noted for his fine acting (21:13-15)—pretended anger and great disappointment. Most certainly he was relieved to be delivered from the prospect of fighting against Israel. The phrase used by Achish, "as Yahweh lives" (29:6), does not imply that Achish was a believer in the God of Israel but was probably used by him to impress David with his sincerity. The designation "your lord" (29:10) is a clear reference to Saul. Possibly Achish was implying by that reference that in dismissing David from the militia he was also being freed from his vassalship to the Philistines. God had sovereignly intervened for David, using the suspicion of the Philistines to deliver him from a rather tight spot.

David's Rescue of the Inhabitants of Ziklag (30:1-31)

The Amalekites, whom Saul had failed to completely destroy (15:2-3, 10-19), continued to be a thorn in the flesh for the Israelites. While David and his men were away with the Philistine militia, Ziklag was attacked and burned by the Amalekites. The women and children were taken captive as slaves (30:2-3). David's warriors were embittered against their leader, apparently concluding that his absence from Ziklag precipitated the disaster. But note that while the people wept away their strength, David "strengthened himself in the LORD his God" (30:6). David knew where to turn in an hour of trouble. Before pursuing the Amalekites, David used the ephod (cf. 14:3, 23:6, 9) to inquire of the Lord concerning the success of the rescue attempt. The Lord graciously assured David that he would overtake the Amalekites and recover *all* that had been lost (30:7-8).

David and his men traveled south to the brook Besor, the major wadi that drains the Negev and empties into the Mediterranean Sea just south of Gaza. There David left two hundred men who were too exhausted by the three-day march from Aphek (30:1) to continue. As they traveled on, David's men discovered an Egyptian slave of the Amalekites who had been left to die in the wilderness (30:11-13). David promised the slave his life for leading him to the camp of the Amalekites (30:15). David's warriors came upon the Amalekites as they were celebrating their successes. They quickly turned the picnic into a panic. Only 400 camel riders escaped the slaughter (30:17). As God had promised, David recovered his wives and *all* that had been taken.

Returning to the two hundred men who had remained at the brook Besor, David was faced with a problem. Some selfish men did not want to divide the spoil with those who had remained with the baggage. David, however, rejected that idea. He argued that the spoil was a gift from Yahweh who had secured their victory over the Amalekites (30:23). He saw to it that the spoil was equitably distributed among those who fought and those who guarded the baggage. That decision demonstrated David's justice and established a precedent that was followed as late as the Maccabean era (see the apocryphal 2 Macc. 8:28-30). David also sent gifts from the spoil to the elders of Judah. That "gift-giving diplomacy" helped David to reestablish his relationships among the leaders of Judah after his sojourn in Philistia. It was the people of Judah who were later to name him king (2 Sam. 2:1-4). The cities mentioned in verses 27-31 were all situated in the territories of Judah and Simeon. *Bethel* refers not to the city in Benjamin, but probably to the *Bethul* of Joshua 19:4. Hebron was among the cities of Judah to receive David's gifts. There he was later anointed king over Israel and ruled for seven and a half years before moving his capital to Jerusalem (2 Sam. 5:1-5).

Saul's Death on Mount Gilboa (31:1-13)

First Samuel concludes with the account of Saul's death and Israel's defeat in fulfillment of Samuel's posthumous prophecy (28:19). As the battle turned against Israel the warriors fled the battlefield and were slain by the Philistines on Mount Gilboa, a 1,696-foot hill in the valley of Jezreel. Saul's sons, including loyal Jonathan, were also slain in battle. Badly wounded by the archers, Saul commanded his armor bearer to take his life, lest he be taken alive and abused by the Philistine warriors (31:3-4). When the armor bearer refused, Saul took his own life by falling on his sword, thus vacating the throne of Israel. Ironically, Saul himself accomplished what David had refused to do—to take the life of the Lord's anointed king. So great was Israel's defeat at the Battle of Gilboa that many of the cities in northern Israel were abandoned as their citizens fled to regions safe from the Philistine menace. As a result, the Philistines came to occupy many Israelite cities (31:7).

When the bodies of Saul and his sons were discovered the next day by the Philistine looters, they were taken to the strategic city of Beth-shan (Tel Bet Shean), located at the junction of the Jezreel and Jordan valleys. There the bodies were put on public display as a means of dishonoring the dead. Although verse 10 indicates that the bodies were hung on the wall, 2 Samuel 21:12 records that they were placed in an open square of the city. Apparently, they were hung *on* a wall *in* an open square of Beth-shan. According to 1 Chronicles 10:10 Saul's head was displayed as a trophy of war in the temple of Dagon. The weapons of Saul were

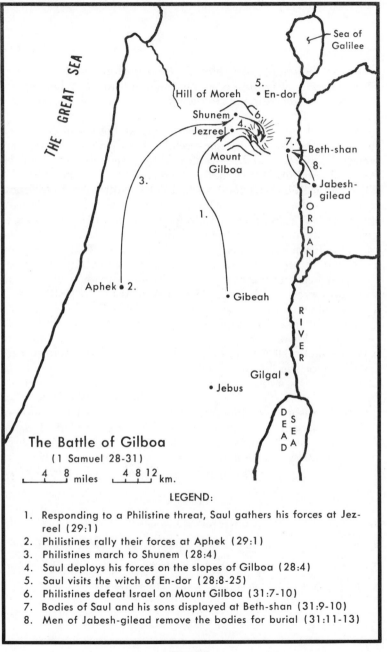

The Battle of Gilboa
(1 Samuel 28-31)

4 8 miles   4 8 12 km.

LEGEND:

1. Responding to a Philistine threat, Saul gathers his forces at Jezreel (29:1)
2. Philistines rally their forces at Aphek (29:1)
3. Philistines march to Shunem (28:4)
4. Saul deploys his forces on the slopes of Gilboa (28:4)
5. Saul visits the witch of En-dor (28:8-25)
6. Philistines defeat Israel on Mount Gilboa (31:7-10)
7. Bodies of Saul and his sons displayed at Beth-shan (31:9-10)
8. Men of Jabesh-gilead remove the bodies for burial (31:11-13)

Fig. 3.2

placed in the temple of Ashtoreth, the Canaanite goddess of fertility and war. *Ashtaroth* is simply the plural form of the Hebrew *Ashtoreth* and corresponds to the Greek *Astarte* and the Mesopotamian *Ishtar*.

When the men of Jabesh-gilead learned how Saul had been dishonored by the public exposure of his body at Beth-shan, they courageously recovered the bodies of Saul and his sons from the city wall and buried them under a tamarisk tree at Jabesh (31:11-13). The men of Jabesh-gilead had not forgotten Saul's kindness to them in the past (cf. 11:1-11) and expressed their debt of gratitude by risking their lives to give Saul and his sons a proper burial. Cremation was not normal Hebrew practice, except in the case of notorious criminals (cf. Gen. 38:24; Lev. 20:14; 21:9; Josh. 7:25).[4] In this instance, the bodies were probably burned because they had been mutilated by the Philistines. Even so, the bones were preserved and buried. The week of fasting (31:13) was a sign of public mourning for the king of Israel.

The great failure of Saul as king was his lack of obedience to the will and word of God (cf. 15:22-23). Although Saul had served Israel well in a military capacity, he was unable to care for the inner conflicts of his own soul and the spiritual problems of his life. His military victories were more than overshadowed by his tragic spiritual failures. It was Saul's disobedience that eventually disqualified him from the office of king. How different the story of Saul's life might read had he obeyed God. His life might have ended in great glory rather than tragic defeat. Christ put the priority of obedience in new perspective when He said, "If you love Me, you will keep My commandments" (John 14:15).

NOTES

1. J. J. Stamm, "Der Name des Königs David," *Supplement to Vetus Testamentum* 7 (1960): 165-83.
2. John J. Davis, *The Birth of a Kingdom* (Winona Lake, Ind.: Brethren Missionary Herald, 1970), p. 88.
3. Yohanan Aharoni and Michael Avi-Yonah, *The Macmillan Bible Atlas* (New York: Macmillan, 1968), p. 64.
4. Roland De Vaux, *Ancient Israel,* 2 vols. (New York: McGraw-Hill, 1965), 1:57.

4

THE TRIUMPHS OF DAVID

2 SAMUEL 1-10

DAVID'S LAMENT FOR SAUL AND JONATHAN (1:1-27)
    The Amalekite's Report of Saul's Death (1:1-16)
    The Lament for Saul and Jonathan (1:17-27)

DAVID'S REIGN OVER JUDAH AT HEBRON (2:1—4:12)
    The Anointing of David as King over Judah (2:1-7)
    The Appointment of Ish-bosheth as King over Israel (2:8-11)
    The Conflict Between Abner and Joab (2:12-32)
    The Defection of Abner to David (3:1-39)
    The Death of Ish-bosheth (4:1-12)

DAVID'S REIGN OVER ALL ISRAEL AT JERUSALEM (5:1—10:19)
    The Establishment of David's Throne (5:1-25)
    The Removal of the Ark to Jerusalem (6:1-23)
    The Establishment of the Davidic Covenant (7:1-29)
    The Conquests of David (8:1-18)
    The Kindness of David to Mephibosheth (9:1-13)
    The Conflict with the Ammonites and Arameans (10:1-19)

4

THE TRIUMPHS OF DAVID

2 SAMUEL 1-10

The book of 2 Samuel continues the story of David's rise to
the throne and records the history of his forty-year rule. It is
there that the reader really gets to know the man David as both
his strengths and weaknesses are revealed. The first ten chapters
record David's successes as he was installed first as king over Judah
at Hebron, then as king over all Israel at Jerusalem. His spiritual
qualifications for kingship are seen in his concern for the Ark and
the house of the Lord (chap. 6-7). David's military qualifications
to lead the nation are evidenced by his successful conquest of the
surrounding nations (chap. 8). The historical record of 2 Samuel
1-10 is paralleled in 1 Chronicles 11-19.

DAVID'S LAMENT FOR SAUL AND JONATHAN (1:1-27)

Second Samuel begins on the same note of tragedy with which
1 Samuel concluded. Saul and his sons had died on Mount Gilboa
defending Israel from the attacking Philistines. The death of Saul
removed the major obstacle to David's rise to kingship. Yet instead of gloating over the demise of his enemy, David lamented
the deaths of Saul, Jonathan, and the men of Israel.

The Amalekite's Report of Saul's Death (1:1-16)

It was three days after his return to Ziklag after defeating the
Amalekites (1 Sam. 30:1-25) that David learned of the deaths of
Saul and Jonathan (1:4). The report came by way of an Amalekite who claimed to have "escaped from the camp of Israel" (1:3).
He was probably a mercenary soldier who had joined Saul's forces
in the battle of Gilboa. In response to David's further inquiry
concerning the deaths of Saul and Jonathan, the Amalekite re-

ported that he had come across the wounded king on the battle-field and had killed him in obedience to Saul's own command (1:6-10). There is a problem in harmonizing the account of 1 Samuel 31:1-6 with the report given David by the Amalekite. There are two possible interpretations. One possibility is that Saul attempted suicide but failed, and the Amalekite simply finished him off. The problem with that approach is that 1 Samuel 31:4-5 indicates that Saul *died* from falling on his sword. It is more likely that Saul died as recorded in 1 Samuel 31:1-6 and that the Amalekite's story was a fabrication. He apparently sought recognition or reward from David for slaying Saul. As a mercenary soldier (or battlefield looter) he came across Saul's body and took Saul's crown and bracelet (1:10) to substantiate his story and thus ingratiate himself to David.

Rather than rejoicing in the death of Saul as the Amalekite probably expected, David tore his clothes as a public sign of mourning (cf. Gen. 37:29, 34). David then joined his men in fasting and weeping for Saul, Jonathan, and the warriors of Israel who had fallen by the swords of the Philistines. David apparently believed the Amalekite's story and had him executed on the basis of his own testimony of having slain Yahweh's anointed king—something David had refused to do on several occasions (1:14-16, cf. 1 Sam. 24, 26).

The Lament for Saul and Jonathan (1:17-27)

David's eulogy over Saul and Jonathan is a poetic description of a national tragedy and an expression of genuine sorrow and grief. David particularly mourned the loss of his loyal friend, Jonathan. The lament begins with a prologue (1:17-18) in which David instructed that the children be taught "the bow" (i.e., the song of the bow), evidently a reference to the ballad that follows. The song was recorded in the book of Jashar. That non-extant volume, also mentioned in Josh. 10:13, may have contained a history of Israel's wars in which some important events and great men were commemorated poetically.

The lament itself (1:19-27) may be divided into three parts based upon the key refrain, "How the mighty have fallen" (1:19, 25, 27). That refrain expresses the burden of the lament. In

88   FIRST AND SECOND SAMUEL

verses 19-24 David praises the fallen heroes. The "high places" (1:19) refer to the heights of Mount Gilboa where Saul and Jonathan died. Shields were normally covered with oil to cleanse, polish, and protect them, but Saul's was not (1:21). His shield was defiled with his own blood and became useless. Yet although they had died in battle, the bow of Jonathan and the sword of Saul did not turn back until they had been satisfied with the blood of the Philistines (1:22). The two heroes were alike in bravery and courage. Jonathan remained loyal to his father in spite of his love for David (1:23). The reference in verse 24 is to the royal apparel that Saul brought to the nation as he became king.

In verses 25-26 David repeats the key refrain and compares Jonathan's love with the love of a woman—a love that is deep and loyal. The lament concludes with a couplet in which the refrain, "How the mighty have fallen," is repeated a third time. The "weapons of war" (1:27) is probably a figurative reference to the fallen warriors.

DAVID'S REIGN OVER JUDAH AT HEBRON (2:1–4:12)

Chapters 2-4 record the conflict between two rivals—David, who took the throne of Judah, and Ish-bosheth, Saul's surviving son, who took the throne in Israel. Ish-bosheth, lacking support, was finally assassinated.

The Anointing of David as King over Judah (2:1-7)

Chapter 2 begins with the record of David's second anointing (cf. 1 Sam. 16:13). In response to the special revelation of Yahweh, David took his family and his followers to live in the city of Hebron. Hebron is located about twenty miles south of Jerusalem, and approximately eighteen miles northeast of Ziklag, where David had been residing (cf. 1 Sam. 27:6-7; 30:1, 26). There at Hebron the men of Judah recognized David's leadership and anointed him king over Judah. His earlier diplomacy in honoring the elders of Judah paid off (cf. 1 Sam. 30:26-30).

It was the men of Judah who reported to David the good deed of the men of Jabesh-gilead who had recovered and buried the body of King Saul (1 Sam. 31:11-13). David recognized the good deed and sought to win the allegiance of the men of Jabesh by promising them a demonstration of his goodness (2:5-6). In his message to Jabesh-gilead David claimed to be Saul's legitimate successor and expressed hope for their strong support of his rule (2:7).

The Appointment of Ish-bosheth as King over Israel (2:8-11)

After Saul's death Abner, commander of Saul's army, took it upon himself to appoint Ish-bosheth, Saul's youngest son, as king over Israel. His name was originally Eshbaal (1 Chron. 8:33; 9: 39), meaning "Baal lives," but was altered to Ish-bosheth ("man of shame") because of his shameful demise. Ish-bosheth was enthroned at Mahanaim, a site located just north of the River Jabbok in Transjordan. There at his new capital Ish-bosheth ruled for two years over the Israelites in northern Israel and Transjordan. While Saul's son ruled in the north, David ruled Judah in the south (2:11). The biblical text records that Ish-bosheth ruled two years, whereas David ruled seven and a half years. A possible explanation for the difference in lengths of reigns is that Ish-bosheth might not have taken the throne immediately. Perhaps he spent the first five years after Saul's death recovering the northern territory that had been conquered by the Philistines.

The Conflict Between Abner and Joab (2:12-32)

It was not long before fighting broke out between the followers of David and the followers of Ish-bosheth. Abner, commander of the northern tribes, and Joab, commander of the armies of Judah, met one day at the pool of Gibeon. The site of Gibeon (el-Jib) is located just seven miles northwest of Jerusalem. The "pool of Gibeon" (2:13) was discovered in the excavation of the site. It measures thirty-seven feet in diameter and thirty-five feet in depth. The pool had a circular staircase that led to a stepped tunnel that continued downward another forty-five feet below the pool's floor to a water chamber.[1] There at the pool Abner proposed a contest between champions in behalf of the opposing armies. Since all twenty-four of the contestants died in combat, the contest was a draw, and a battle between the two armies ensued (2:15-17). The name *Helkath-hazzurim* ("the field of sword edges") was given to the site to commemorate the contest at Gibeon.

Verses 18-23 record the slaying of Asahel, Joab's brother, by Abner. When Asahel began pursuing Abner, commander of Ish-bosheth's forces, he was warned twice to turn aside. Apparently Abner wanted to avoid a blood feud, which might develop from his killing Joab's brother. When he saw that a confrontation could not be avoided, Abner was forced to slay Asahel (2:23).

In order to put an end to the bloodshed, Abner called for a truce (2:24-26). Joab was willing to cease hostilities, but blamed Abner for suggesting combat in the first place (2:14, 27). Had Abner not issued a challenge, the conflict would have been avoided altogether. After a truce was arranged, Abner and his men returned to Mahanaim. The count of the dead and missing indicates that Joab was clearly the victor in the battle (2:30-31). Whereas Abner had lost 360 men, Joab lost only nineteen.

The Defection of Abner to David (3:1-39)

When Ish-bosheth accused Abner of disloyalty, the powerful commander decided to defect to David and unify Israel under his rule. Chapter 3 records his defection and his assassination by Joab. The chapter highlights David's response to Abner's death. It is clear from the record that it was not David's desire to secure the northern kingdom by intrigue or murder.

The chapter begins by recording the names of the sons born to David while he was residing at Hebron (3:2-5). Sons born to him at Jerusalem are named in 5:13-16 (cf. 1 Chron. 3:1-9). The six wives mentioned here reflect David's involvement in marriage alliances with foreign powers. Marriage alliances between royal houses were quite common in the ancient Near East. They served to confirm treaties and cement relationships between the two states concerned.[2] That type of marriage was, of course, forbidden by Mosaic law (Deut. 7:3; 17:17) as were covenants with foreign nations (Exod. 23:32; 34:12; Deut. 7:12). The marriage alliance with Talmai, king of Geshur (3:3) was probably aimed against the northern tribes' loyalty to Ish-bosheth. The alliance gained David an ally to the north of Ish-bosheth's kingdom, placing him in a precarious position between Geshur (northeast of the Sea of Galilee) and Judah.

Verses 6-11 reveal that Abner, commander of the armies of

Israel, was the real power behind the throne in the northern kingdom. Abner was charged by Ish-bosheth with having sexual relations with Saul's concubine, Rizpah. In ancient times a concubine was a slave woman who was the legal chattel of her master
and often served to raise him an heir. By the time of the monarchy the possession of concubines appears to have been a royal
prerogative. Having intercourse with a king's concubine was a
serious offense, for it was in essence making a claim for the throne
(cf. 16:20-22; 1 Kings 2:13-25). Abner does not deny the charges
but refutes Ish-bosheth's veiled suggestion that the affair with
Rizpah was politically motivated. He questions, "Am I a dog's
head that belongs to Judah?" (3:8). That is, "Am I a contemptible
traitor?" In a fit of anger Abner vowed to transfer the kingdom
of Saul to David so that David might rule from Dan to Beersheba—from the northern to the southern border of Israel. Although Abner's death prevented his fulfillment of the vow, the immediate steps he took show that he had the power and authority
to carry it out.

Abner immediately began negotiations with David, but before
agreeing to enter a covenant with Abner, David demanded the
return of his wife Michal (1 Sam. 18:27) whom Saul had given
to another man (1 Sam. 25:44). Abner agreed to the condition,
and Michal was returned to David despite the protests of her second husband (3:14-16). Through the return of Michal, David
was able to reestablish relations with Saul's family—an important
step to being recognized as successor to Saul's throne in Israel.

True to his word Abner began to drum up support for David
among the elders of the northern kingdom and the people of Benjamin (3:17-18). When he went to Hebron to report the results
of his campaign to David, Abner and the men with him were honored at an official state dinner (3:20-21). Joab, commander of
David's army, did not return to Hebron until after Abner's departure. Only then did he learn of the negotiations between David
and Abner. He immediately accused Abner of treachery against
David (3:25) and then took matters into his own hands. He sent
messengers to call Abner back to Hebron and then deceitfully
struck him down at the city gate (3:26-27). Apparently Abishai
played a part in the assassination (3:30). The writer records that

Abner died on account of Joab's brother, Asahel (cf. 2:18-23).
However, no approval of this evil deed is implied. Hebron was
a city of refuge (Josh. 20:7) and not even a blood avenger could
slay a murderer there without a trial (Num. 35:10-28). It is probable that the slaying of Abner was also politically motivated. Joab
did not want a high-ranking officer from Saul's army threatening
his position as commander of David's troops.

Recognizing the wrong done to Abner, David was quick to af-
firm his innocence of any wrongdoing (3:28). Yet although David
pronounced a strong curse on Joab and his family, he failed to discipline his chief army officer. David demonstrated his sincere
sorrow over Abner's death by (1) tearing his clothes, (2) lament-
ing Abner's undeserved death, and (3) fasting until sunset (3:31-
35). David's public mourning made it clear to the people of the
northern kingdom that it was not his desire to put Abner to death
(3:37).

The Death of Ish-bosheth (4:1-12)

Chapter 4 records how Ish-bosheth lost power and was slain by
two of his own men, who then defected to David. When Ish-
bosheth learned that Abner had been slain, he lost confidence (literally, "his hands dropped"), and that had repercussions throughout Israel. It was not long before two commanders in Saul's army
planned and carried out the assassination of the king. The paren-
thesis in 2b-3 explains how those brothers were Benjamites, yet had
descended from Rimmon of Beeroth (el-bire). Although Beeroth
was outside the original tribal territory of Benjamin, the city was
taken over by the Benjamites when abandoned by its earlier inhabitants. Although verse 4 interrupts the narrative, it reveals
that Saul had a surviving son, Mephibosheth, who had been crippled as a result of an accident following the battle of Gilboa
(1 Sam. 31:1-7). The name of Saul's youngest son was originally
Merib-baal ("Baal strives"), but was corrupted to Mephibosheth
("he scatters shame") to avoid idolatrous implications. That reference to Saul's surviving descendant lays the foundation for the
events of chapter 9.

The assassination of Ish-bosheth by Rechab and Baanah took
place while the king was taking his midday rest. The assassins

apparently entered the house pretending to be wheat carriers and killed Ish-bosheth while he was resting on his bed. They then fled the kingdom and traveled by way of the Arabah—the desolate area north of the Dead Sea—to Hebron. When the murderers presented David with the head of Ish-bosheth, they undoubtedly expected to be rewarded, but were instead executed (4:8-12). In verse 11 David calls Ish-bosheth a "righteous" man, for he was not guilty of any wicked deed or crime. He had merely assumed the throne upon Saul's death at the encouragement of Abner. The mutilation and exposure of the assassins' bodies served as a public denouncement of their evil deed (cf. Deut. 21:22). Although David rightly recognized the guilt of the assassins, God was clearly in control of those events. The sovereign God of Israel allowed the evil actions of those evil men to accomplish His will, for the death of Ish-bosheth cleared the way for David to be anointed king over all Israel (cf. 5:3).

DAVID'S REIGN OVER ALL ISRAEL AT JERUSALEM (5:1—10:19)

Chapters 5-10 recount the prosperity and divine blessing David enjoyed as he reigned over all Israel at Jerusalem. After seven and a half years of division and disunity the kingdom was consolidated under David, who ruled the united kingdoms of Israel and Judah for the next thirty-three years. It was during those early years of prosperity that David brought the Ark to Jerusalem, conceived of plans to build the Temple, and expanded his kingdom to the north, south, east, and west (8:1-14). David's conquests and alliances gave him control of territory from the River of Egypt (the wadi el-'Arish) to the Euphrates. Truly, those were David's years of triumph. The key to David's success as king is revealed in 5:10, "And David became greater and greater, for the LORD God of hosts was with him."

The Establishment of David's Throne (5:1-25)

After the death of Ish-bosheth the elders of the tribes of Israel came to David at Hebron, acknowledging his right to rule over the entire nation. They clearly recognized that it was God's will for David to shepherd Israel as king (5:2). Verse 3 records David's third anointing (cf. 2:4; 1 Sam. 16:13), which resulted in the unification of the twelve tribes under one king. The "forty" years of verse 4 is a rounded figure. Verse 5 indicates that David reigned a total of forty and a half years as king.

David's first tasks as king were to eliminate the foreign wedge between the northern and southern tribes and to establish his capital in a neutral area. Both objectives were accomplished with the conquest of the Jebusite fortress at Jerusalem. Jebus, situated near the border of Judah and Benjamin, was an excellent fortress city because the surrounding deep valleys made it naturally defensible on three sides. In addition, it had a good water supply—the Gihon spring—and was close to travel routes for trade. Although the Jebusites, of Canaanite descent (Gen. 10:16-18), boasted that the blind and the lame could defend Jerusalem, the fortress was captured as David's men entered the water tunnel that went under the walls into the city (5:8; cf. 1 Chron. 11:6). The name *Zion* (probably derived from the Semitic root *syn*, "to protect") is used to refer to the stronghold that David's men captured. Since David dwelt there, it also came to be called, "the city of David" (cf. 1 Chron. 11:5-7). After the capture of the fortress David took immediate steps to further fortify the city. He built Millo (from "to fill," hence "a mound") to serve as part of Jerusalem's northern defenses since the city was most open to attack from that direction.

International recognition of David's rule over Israel came quickly. Soon Hiram, King of Tyre, sent messengers to begin negotiations with David. He also sent skilled Phoenician workmen to build David a fine house (5:11). That was a political and economic move for Hiram. He could profit from trade with Israel and was especially in need of Israel's grain (cf. 1 Kings 5:11; Acts 12:20).

The multiplication of David's wives and concubines (5:13-16) was in direct violation of Deut. 17:17. These verses reflect David's involvement in international treaties and alliances that were sealed by the marriage of a king's daughter to the other participants in the treaty. That cultural institution accounts for some of David's and Solomon's many wives (cf. 1 Kings 11:1-3).

It was not long before the Philistines realized that David was no longer their vassal and took decisive military action against the new capital. Twice the Philistines advanced toward Jerusalem through the valley of Rephaim, the most direct approach to Jerusalem from Philistia. Upon hearing of the Philistine mobilization David went down to the stronghold (i.e., Jerusalem, 5:7) to inquire of the Lord concerning the outcome of the battle. Being assured of victory, David fought his first battle with the Philistines at Baal-perazim, "the lord of breaking through," which they named the site as a result of the outcome of the battle. The image inherent in the name is that of flooding waters breaking through a dam, as David's troops had broken through the Philistine assault. The idols that the Philistines had taken into battle to assure them victory were captured as trophies of war by the Israelites. In keeping with David's instructions, the idols were later burned (1 Chron. 14:12).

The Philistines did not easily give up on David, their former vassal. Once again they advanced up the valley of Rephaim. This time the Lord instructed David to instigate a counter attack, surprising the Philistines from behind (5:23). The sound of stepping movements on the tops of the balsam trees (or Baka-shrubs), where the Israelites were waiting under cover, was to be a sign to them of Yahweh's coming upon the battlefield to strike down the Philistine (5:24). Because of the Lord the Israelites won another great victory and the Philistines were driven out of the hill country (5:25). With the nearby Philistine opposition subdued, David was free to take future steps to convert his fledgling kingdom into an empire.

The Removal of the Ark to Jerusalem (6:1-23)

Unlike Saul, David was intensely interested in the worship of Yahweh and gave attention to the Ark, which had been neglected during the reign of his predecessor. David took thirty thousand of his men to Baale-Judah ("Lords of Judah"), also known as Kiriath-jearim (1 Sam. 7:1-2), in order to escort the Ark to Jerusalem. Verse 2 reveals that the Ark represented the glorious reputation ("name") and gracious presence ("sitting") of Yahweh of Hosts (cf. 1 Sam. 1:3) in Israel.

In the first attempt to bring the Ark to Jerusalem (6:1-11), two violations of Old Testament law took place. First, the Ark was

carried on an ox cart. That violated the Old Testament requirement
that the Ark be *carried* by the sons of Kohath (Exod. 25:14-15;
Num. 3:30-31; 7:9), not transported by a cart or other vehicle. In
his enthusiasm for moving the Ark to Jerusalem as quickly as possible, David adopted a Philistine expedient (1 Sam. 6:7-8). The
second violation of Old Testament law took place when Uzzah inadvertently touched the Ark to keep it from toppling off the cart.
Touching the Ark was in direct violation of Numbers 4:15. The
sin of Uzzah in touching the Ark (6:6-7) resulted from the fact
that the Ark was not being carried by the Levites as God had
directed. That violation of God's holiness cost Uzzah his life.
David's anger over the incident (6:8) was probably directed at
himself rather than toward the Lord since the calamity resulted
from his own carelessness. Filled with anger and fear, David left
the Ark at the house of Obed-edom, the Gittite (a former resident
of Gath). The judgment on Uzzah serves as a warning against
"situation ethics." Because of His holiness, God's laws cannot be
violated no matter how reasonable it would seem in a particular
situation.

In David's second attempt to bring the Ark to Jerusalem (6:12-
23), it was transported in the manner prescribed by the Old Testament law (6:13). David expressed his joy over the coming of
the Ark to Jerusalem by dancing (6:14, 16)—literally, "whirling
around." For the occasion David was attired in a linen ephod—a
sleeveless priestly garment extending to the hips and used while
officiating before the altar (1 Sam. 2:18, 28). Although David was
not a Levite he officiated as a priest and is typical of Christ who is
both a king and a priest (cf. Zech. 6:12-13).

Michal's contempt for David (6:16) at that exciting celebration
is evidenced by her sarcastic remark in verse 20. She considered
David's conduct as unbefitting for a king. Her mention of David
as being "uncovered" is probably a derogatory reference to the
priestly attire that he wore (cf. 6:14). David rebuked Michal for
her attitude and expressed his willingness to be lowly esteemed, for
it is the humble whom the Lord will exalt (6:22; cf. 1 Sam. 7:7-8;
Matt. 23:12). Verse 23 may mean that David ceased to have marriage relations with Michal as a punishment for her haughtiness.

But the context suggests that her childless condition was *divine* discipline for Michal's contempt of David, the anointed king. Michal's childlessness prevented her from providing a successor to the throne from the family of Saul (cf. 6:21).

The Establishment of the Davidic Covenant (7:1-29)

Second Samuel 7 records the establishment of the Davidic Covenant—God's unconditional promise to David and his posterity that they would receive an eternal house, an eternal throne, and an eternal kingdom (7:16). That promise is an important key to our understanding of God's prophetic program. Having settled down in his beautiful new palace (cf. 5:11) and enjoyed a period of rest from war (7:1), David began to concern himself with finding a permanent resting place for the Ark of God. David felt that it was inappropriate for him to be enjoying such a fine palace while the Ark of God was being kept in a tent. Nathan, David's prophetic counselor, concurred and encouraged David to pursue the project he had in mind with the Lord's blessing (7:3).

Later that evening the Lord spoke to Nathan and instructed him that David would not build Him a house. Rather, God would build David a "house"—that is, a dynasty (7:11). There are at least three reasons why David's plan to build a permanent resting place for the Ark is rejected. First, since the Exodus, the Ark had been in a tent (7:6). There was no pressing need to change that arrangement. Second, God had simply not asked for a house (7:7). Third, although there would some day be a Temple, David would not be the one to build it, because he had waged wars and shed blood (7:5; cf. 1 Chron. 22:8; 28:3). It would be Solomon, the man of peace, who would eventually build God's house (1 Kings 6:1).

The Lord went on to reveal His plan and purposes for David. As He had blessed David in the past (7:8-9a), so He would bless him in the future (7:9b-11). That future blessing included building David a great house—an everlasting dynasty. The Davidic Covenant (7:12-16) is based upon God's promise to Abraham in Genesis 12:1-3 where the patriarch and his descendants are promised a land, a nation, and a blessing. Although the land promise is developed in the Palestinian Covenant (Deut. 30:1-10), and the blessing promised is developed in the New Covenant (Jer. 31:31-34), the promise of a nation is amplified and confirmed in the Davidic Covenant of 2 Samuel 7:12-16.

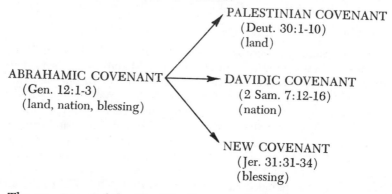

PALESTINIAN COVENANT
(Deut. 30:1-10)
(land)

ABRAHAMIC COVENANT
(Gen. 12:1-3)
(land, nation, blessing)

DAVIDIC COVENANT
(2 Sam. 7:12-16)
(nation)

NEW COVENANT
(Jer. 31:31-34)
(blessing)

The provisions of the Davidic Covenant include: (1) David will have a son and successor for whom God will establish a kingdom, 7:12; (2) David's son (Solomon) would build the Temple instead of David, 7:13a; (3) The throne of Solomon's kingdom will be established forever, 7:13b; (4) Though his sins justify chastening, the right to the throne will never be taken away from the Davidic dynasty, 7:14-15; (5) David's house, throne, and kingdom will endure forever, 7:16. In other words, the line of David would always be the royal line with the right to the throne and the right to a literal, earthly kingdom. It is important to note that the covenant did not guarantee that the rule by David's posterity would be uninterrupted, for indeed it was when Judah was taken into exile (2 Kings 25). However, the prerogative to exercise the privilege of ruling would always belong to the Davidic dynasty.

Luke 1:32-33 reveals the one with whom God will eventually fulfill His covenant promises—David's descendant, Jesus Christ. In Luke 1:32-33 the angel Gabriel tells Mary that the Lord God will give to Jesus "the *throne* of His father David; and He will reign over the *house* of Jacob forever, and His *kingdom* will have no end" (italics added). Jesus is promised an eternal throne, house, and kingdom—exactly what God promised David and his posterity. The ultimate fulfillment of the covenant provisions then must take place at the second advent when Christ returns to reign over David's kingdom.

There are at least five prophetic implications of God's promise to David in 2 Samuel 7:12-16.[3] They are: (1) Israel must be preserved as a nation (cf. Jer. 31:35-36); (2) Israel must be brought back to their land (cf. Deut. 30:1-5); (3) David's Son, Jesus the Messiah, must return to rule over the covenanted kingdom (cf. Rev. 19:11-16); (4) A literal, earthly kingdom for Israel must be instituted, over which Christ will reign (cf. Rev. 20:1-4); and (5) The kingdom must become an eternal kingdom (cf. 1 Cor. 15:24). Since God's promise to David was unconditional, the future fulfillment of those events is certain.

The prayer prayed by David after receiving the word from the Lord exemplifies the proper response of a believer to God's revealed will. Instead of complaining about the fact that he would be unable to build God a temple, David rejoiced in the promise of future blessing and acknowledged God's greatness (7:18-24). He concludes his prayer with a petition that God will confirm the covenant forever in order that Yahweh's name might be forever magnified (7:25-29). David's request for God's blessing (7:29) reflects his concern that his descendants would be faithful to the trust committed to them.

The Conquests of David (8:1-18)

Chapter 8 outlines the expansion of David's kingdom under the prospering hand of the Lord. Israel's major enemies were all defeated as the empire and fame of David extended north, south, east, and west. David's expansionist policies were probably due in part to his concern to protect Israelite settlements in Transjordan. The key to David's success is revealed in verse 6, "the LORD helped David wherever he went."

One of David's first priorities was to deal with the Philistine menace to the west. He quickly defeated and subjugated the Philistines and took control of their "chief city," probably Gath (cf. 1 Chron. 18:1). He also defeated the Moabites in Transjordan and required that they bring him tribute in acknowledgment of his rule. That represents a change from the good relationship David once enjoyed with the Moabite royalty (cf. 1 Sam. 22:3-4). Verse

2 may be understood to mean that David spared the *young* Moabites (whose height was approximately one cord) and executed the *adults* (whose height was two cords). On the other hand, it may be that one out of three rows of soldiers was arbitrarily chosen to be spared from execution.

David's campaigns to the north resulted in the defeat of the king of Zobah (8:3-4), the Arameans of Damascus (8:5-8), and the submission of the king of Hamath (8:9-11). "Zobah" (8:3) refers to an Aramean kingdom north of Damascus. The king was defeated, not the son of the king. Verse 5 clearly indicates that Hadadezer was the king of Zobah whom David defeated. The expression "son of Rehob" (lit., *ben Rehob*) is used like a last name. Hadadezer, the son of Rehob, was the king of Zobah (v. 3). The number "seventeen hundred horsemen" (8:4) is apparently a scribal error in transmission, for the Septuagint and 1 Chron. 18:4 indicate the text should read, "one thousand chariots and seven thousand horsemen." Hamstringing the horses disabled them from military action by cutting the back sinews of the hind legs. Since Syria did not exist as a political entity until the Hellenistic period (332 B.C.–63 B.C.), it is better to refer to the Old Testament region as *Aram* and the people as *Arameans*, as does the Hebrew text (8:5-6). *Betah* (8:8) is an Aramean city also known as Tibhath (cf. 1 Chron. 18:8). Hamath (8:9), another Aramean state, was located about 100 miles north of Damascus. Toi, king of Hamath, was no doubt happy to see Zobah crushed and desired to establish friendly relations with his powerful new neighbor. The gifts he gave David may indicate that he voluntarily submitted to David as his vassal (8:10-11).

David's campaigns to the south resulted in the defeat and subjugation of the Edomites, descendants of Esau (8:13-14). Verse 13 contains a textual problem representing a scribal error in transmission. The reference is probably to David's defeat of the Edomites, not the Arameans. That is indicated by Psalm 60:1 and 1 Chron. 18:12, which record that it was the Edomites who were defeated by David in the Valley of Salt, south of the Dead Sea. The chapter concludes with a brief note concerning the administration and ministers serving in David's kingdom (8:15-18).

As a result of David's conquests the sovereignty of Israel ex-

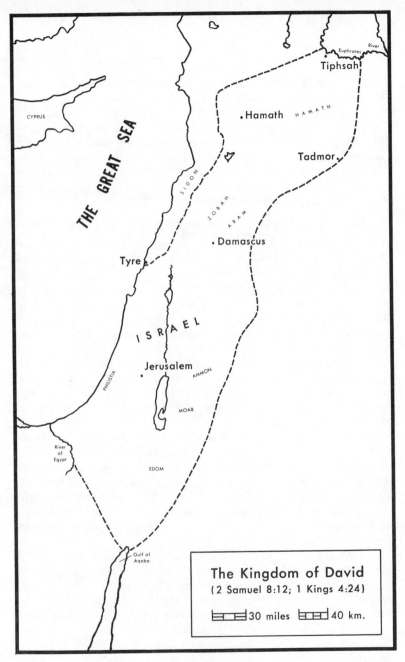

CYPRUS

THE GREAT SEA

Euphrates River

•Tiphsah

•Hamath   HAMATH

Tadmor•

SIDON

ZOBAH

ARAM

•Damascus

Tyre•

I S R A E L

•Jerusalem

AMMON

PHILISTIA

MOAB

River of Egypt

EDOM

Gulf of Aqaba

The Kingdom of David
(2 Samuel 8:12; 1 Kings 4:24)

30 miles   40 km.

Fig. 4.1

tended from the Gulf of Aqaba and the River of Egypt (Wadi el-'Arish) to the Euphrates River—the very area God promised Abraham in Gen. 15:18. Was the land promise of the Abrahamic Covenant (Gen. 12:1-3) fulfilled in David's day? No. The nations were David's vassals, but he did not personally possess the land. Although David exercised sovereignty over the land for some time, God promised Abraham's descendants *permanent* possession of the land (Gen. 13:15). The land promises of the Abrahamic Covenant have not yet been fulfilled.

The Kindness of David to Mephibosheth (9:1-13)

Chapter 9 records how David displayed covenant loyalty toward Jonathan (1 Sam. 20:42) by ministering to the physical needs of his crippled son, Mephibosheth. Desiring to show kindness to Saul's family for Jonathan's sake, David inquired as to whether or not there was a surviving descendant upon whom he could grant favor. The word *kindness* (9:1, 3) is related to the Hebrew word for stork and suggests both love and loyalty. It may best be translated "loyal love." David learned from Ziba, a former servant of Saul, that Jonathan's crippled son, Mephibosheth (4:4), was living in Transjordan at Lo-debar. Lo-debar has been identified with Umm ed-Debar, a site located in Gilead about ten miles south of the Sea of Galilee. David immediately sent for Mephibosheth to be brought to Jerusalem (9:5).

When David promised Mephibosheth the restoration of all Saul's land *and* the privilege of eating regularly at the king's table (9:7), Mephibosheth recognized that that favor was undeserved. He questioned, "What is your servant, that you should regard a dead dog like me?" A "dead dog" (9:8) was considered contemptible and useless. Mephibosheth knew that he had not merited David's kindness and that there was no way for him to repay it. David's offer was the expression of sheer grace.

David's expression of loyal love toward Jonathan was prompted by two concerns: (1) the covenant David made with Jonathan as recorded in 1 Sam. 20:42; 23:18, and (2) David's desire to end conflict between his household and the household of Saul. As promised, David returned to Mephibosheth Saul's land (9:10) and made him a permanent guest in the royal dining room (9:13). Verse 10 indicates that although David would provide the necessities of life for Mephibosheth, he would make provision for his own family and servants by cultivating the land that David had returned to him (9:12).

The Conflict with the Ammonites and Arameans (10:1-19)

Chapter 10 records the details of 8:12 concerning David's campaigns against the Ammonites and Arameans. Upon hearing of the death of Nahash, king of the Ammonites, David sent messengers of consolation to Hanun his son. The hostility between Saul and Nahash (1 Sam. 11:1-11) forms the background for that message of consolation. Since Nahash was an enemy of Saul, he was viewed as a friend and supporter of David (10:2). However, David's messengers were accused of espionage and greatly humiliated by Hanun. He shaved the beards of the Hebrews and left them indecently exposed by cutting off their garments at the hips (10:4). Shaving off a person's beard is still regarded by the Arabs today as a great indignity.

When the Ammonites learned that they had offended David, they hired thirty-three thousand mercenary soldiers from the north to join with them in the forthcoming battle against Israel (10:6). In that first confrontation Joab and Abishai skillfully divided their forces and out-manuevered the Ammonite-Aramean coalition (10:7-14), thus bringing Israel a great victory. In the second campaign Hadadezer of Zobah (8:5) enlisted the support of the Arameans beyond the Euphrates. The armies engaged each other at Helam (in Transjordan northeast of Ramoth-gilead) where Israel won another victory (10:15-18). As a result, the Arameans became subject to Israel and feared to help Ammon any more (10:19). In verse 18 the number "seven hundred charioteers" is probably a copyist's error for seven thousand" (cf. 1 Chron. 19:18).

Chapters 9 and 10 show God's blessing on David's demonstration of loyal love. David expressed covenant loyalty to God (chap. 6-7), his fellowman (9:1), and to a foreigner (10:2), which resulted in God's blessing on his rule. That is remarkable in contrast to the judgment on David's sin beginning in chapter 11.

NOTES

1. Howard F. Vos, *Archaeology in Bible Lands* (Chicago: Moody, 1977), pp. 171-72.
2. A. Malamat, "Aspects of the Foreign Policies of David and Solomon," *Journal of Near Eastern Studies* (1963), p. 8.
3. J. Dwight Pentecost, *Things to Come* (Grand Rapids: Zondervan, 1958), pp. 114-15.

5

THE TROUBLES OF DAVID

2 SAMUEL 11-20

DAVID'S GREAT SIN (11:1—12:31)
David's Sin Committed with Bathsheba (11:1-27)
David's Sin Revealed and Judged (12:1-31)

ABSALOM'S MURDER OF AMNON (13:1—14:33)
The Violation of Tamar by Amnon (13:1-19)
The Slaying of Amnon by Absalom (13:20-29)
The Retreat of Absalom to Geshur (13:30-39)
The Return of Absalom to Jerusalem (14:1-33)

ABSALOM'S REBELLION (15:1—18:33)
The Conspiracy of Absalom (15:1-12)
The Flight of David from Jerusalem (15:13—16:14)
The Counsel of Ahithophel and Hushai (16:15—17:23)
The Defeat of Absalom's Army (17:24—18:8)
The Death of Absalom (18:9-18)
The Report of Victory and Absalom's Death (18:18-33)

DAVID'S REINSTATEMENT AS KING (19:1—20:26)
Judah Calls David Back as King (19:1-14)
David Met by His Supporters (19:15-40)
Sheba's Rebellion Suppressed by Joab (19:41—20:22)
David's Chief Officers (20:23-26)

5

THE TROUBLES OF DAVID

2 SAMUEL 11-20

Chapters 11-20 of 2 Samuel record David's troubles in the areas of morals, politics, and family relationships. For David those were years of trouble and turmoil. Although David was a man after God's "own heart" (1 Sam. 13:14), he was not immune to temptation and sin. Yet when he did fall, David was quick to acknowledge his failure, and God was just as quick to forgive the repentant sinner (2 Sam. 12:13). Nevertheless, David learned that sin, even though forgiven, bears serious consequences (cf. James 1:15). As Paul warns, "Do not be deceived, God is not mocked; for whatever a man sows, this he will also reap" (Gal. 6:7). Second Samuel 11-20 illustrates vividly from David's experience the inevitable and devastating consequences of sin in the life of a believer.

DAVID'S GREAT SIN (11:1–12:31)

The Lord never blinks at sin, even when it is found in the life of an otherwise exemplary believer. Chapters 11-12 mark a real low point in David's career as he, at an unguarded moment, yielded to temptation and committed adultery with Bathsheba. As is often the case, one sin led to another, and soon David was guilty both of adultery and murder. These chapters serve as a warning that even a godly man can succumb to temptation and mar an otherwise untainted testimony (cf. 1 Kings 15:5).

David's Sin Committed With Bathsheba (11:1-27)

The occasion of David's sin is quite instructive. It happened in the spring of the year when kings normally went out to battle because of the good weather and abundance of food available along the way. However, while the Israelite forces were besieging the

Ammonite capital of Rabbah (modern 'Amman; cf. 10:1-14), David was at home in Jerusalem. He found himself with time on his hands and soon got involved in moral problems. Beware of having lots of free time available and no constructive plan as to how to use it. In such a situation the mind often wanders, and that gives Satan a strategic opportunity to introduce tempting thoughts and situations. Walking on the roof of his house during a sleepless night David spotted a beautiful woman bathing below. Was Bathsheba guilty of immodesty? Oriental homes had an enclosed courtyard that was considered part of the house. Bathsheba, bathing by lamplight, would not be considered immodest in consideration of the fact that she was in her own house. But she was probably indiscreet. She undoubtedly knew that the interior of her courtyard could be seen from the roof of David's house situated at a higher elevation on Mt. Zion. In the darkness of the night, perhaps David saw more with his imagination than he did with his eye. Both were guilty—Bathsheba for indiscretion and David for fantasizing a relationship with another man's wife.

There were three steps in the process of David's sin: (1) he saw; (2) he inquired; and (3) he yielded to temptation (11:2-4). That process of sin is revealed in James 1:14-15. David was carried away by his *lust*, and that gave birth to *sin*, which resulted in *judgment*. After the purification required by Mosaic law following intercourse (Lev. 15:18), Bathsheba returned to her house.

When David learned that Bathsheba had conceived he attempted to cover up his sin by calling her husband Uriah home from the battlefield (11:6-13). Though a Hittite, Uriah was evidently a worshiper of Yahweh, for his name means "Yahweh is my light." Possibly he was a mercenary soldier who had come to believe in the God of Israel. David encouraged Uriah to go down to his house and visit his wife. The expression, "wash your feet" (11:8) is an idiom of time meaning, "spend some time at home." Uriah is the epitome of dedication to his men and his mission. He refused to relax during a time of war (11:11). Even David's attempt to entice Uriah to alcoholic indulgence failed. Uriah refused to take the liberty offered to him and remained at the king's house.

Failing to cover up his sin with Bathsheba, David plotted the murder of Uriah (11:14-16). Perhaps David was afraid of being accused by Uriah for violating his wife (Lev. 20:10). Perhaps he could not face the shame of seeing Uriah after the warrior learned that his wife was pregnant with David's child. It is ironic that the letter containing David's plan to do away with Uriah was carried to Joab by Uriah himself. As planned, Uriah was sent to the front line and killed in the heat of battle (11:17). The report of Uriah's death brought David no joy—only temporary relief from the prospect of his sin being discovered (11:18-25). After Bathsheba had mourned the death of her husband, David took her as his own wife. Verse 27 reveals that although David had concealed his sin from the general public, the omniscient Yahweh knew all about the whole evil affair. That brief comment sets the stage for chapter 12.

David's Sin Revealed and Judged (12:1-31)

Second Samuel 12 provides the historical background of Psalm 51. Here it is recorded how Nathan the prophet used a very pointed parable to lead David to condemn his own actions and bring him to repentance. Nathan, David's prophetic counselor, was faced with the task of confronting David with his sin. His earlier message to David had been one of divine blessing (7:8-16), but now he must proclaim a message of judgment. Nathan used a parable about a ewe lamb to reveal David's sin (12:1-4). David's pronouncement of judgment on the rich man who took the poor man's lamb is ironic. He declared, "As Yahweh lives, surely the man who has done this deserves to die!" In fact, David was deserving of death for adultery (Lev. 20:10) and murder (Lev. 24:17). David also demanded that restitution be made to the poor man according to Mosaic law (Exod. 22:1).

The words of Nathan, "You are the man!" must have pierced David's heart like the thrust of a hot lance (12:7). Nathan proceeded to apply the parable to David, naming his sins of adultery and murder, which were both an evidence of David's contempt for God's Word (12:9). Note that although David did not personally kill Uriah, he was just as guilty since he instigated the plot and gave the order. Although David's own sword was clean, there was blood on his hands. The judgment pronounced on David and his family is twofold: (1) David's own family would bring evil against him, and (2) David's wives would be taken by another (12:11-12). The second judgment is a veiled reference to the fact that David would lose his throne to an usurper (cf. 3:7-8; 1 Kings 2:13-15). Those predictions of judgment were fulfilled in the violation of Tamar (13:11-14), the violent deaths of Amnon and Absalom (13:38-39; 18:15), and Absalom's public appropriation of David's royal concubines during his rebellion (16:22).

David, the man after God's own heart, did not attempt to rationalize or justify his sin. For that he must be commended. When confronted with the facts, David's confession was immediate— as was God's gracious forgiveness (12:13). The fuller confession of David is found in Psalm 51. Although the sin was forgiven, God declared that the offspring of that adulterous relationship must die in order to vindicate His reputation for righteousness among the nations (12:14). God could not ignore David's sin and thus let unbelievers impugn the holiness of His character. This tragic record shows that although sin is forgiven, sin's inevitable consequences frequently come to fruition in the lives of believers (Gal. 6:7).

As God had promised, the child born to David by Bathsheba became sick and died (12:15-19). David's response to the word concerning the child's death surprised his servants (12:21). His explanation in verse 23 has been thought to support the view that infants and children who die are taken to heaven. But the issue in the context does not concern afterlife, but the inevitability of death. The child could not return to life and activity, but David would some day join his son in death. The point of the verse is that there was no further need for David's fasting since the child had died. Although the Word of God sheds little light on the eternal state of dead infants, there is great comfort in knowing that God's plan must be as perfect as His character—infinitely righteous, loving, and just.

The second son born to David and Bathsheba was Solomon. The name *Jedidiah* ("beloved of Yahweh"), given him by Nathan, marked Solomon as the successor to David's throne (12:24-25; 1 Kings 1:11-30).

The rest of the chapter records how David captured Rabbah and defeated the Ammonites (10:1-14; 13:26-31). There are two views concerning David's treatment of the Ammonites in verse 31. It is possible that he imposed *hard labor* on the captives. However, the verse would require changing "push through" to "toil at," and would contradict 1 Chron. 20:3, which indicates that the Ammonites were cut with saws. The second view is that he imposed *cruel death* on the captives in accordance with Ammonite ways (cf. 1 Sam. 11:2; Amos 1:13). The latter view is probably correct, though the action may have been carried out against only the warriors of the fortified cities that resisted David.

ABSALOM'S MURDER OF AMNON (13:1—14:33)

Chapters 13-14 record the murder of Amnon by his brother Absalom. When Amnon, David's oldest son (3:2), raped his half-sister Tamar, Absalom retaliated by murdering Amnon two years later. Those tragedies within David's family are clearly in fulfillment of God's promised judgment on David for his sin with Bathsheba (12:11). It is noteworthy that the whole episode of Absalom's rebellion (15-18) began with the same sins of which David had been guilty—sexual immorality leading to murder.

The Violation of Tamar by Amnon (13:1-19)

Amnon and Tamar were David's children by Ahinoam and Maacah respectively (3:2-3). Although Amnon's passion was aroused for his half-sister, he found it "hard" to have his desires satisfied (13:2). Marriage to one's sister was forbidden by Levitical law (Lev. 18:11), and he was apparently unable to seduce her. Jonadab, Amnon's shrewd cousin, conceived of a plan by which Tamar could be lured into his bedroom (13:3-5). By pretending to be ill, Amnon was able to get Tamar into his bedroom, and there he raped her. Tamar resisted Amnon and told him to speak to the king, who would not withhold her from him (13:13). Although the law forbade incestuous marriage (Lev. 18:11), that regulation may not have been always strictly observed. Possibly Tamar made the suggestion in hopes of escaping the immediate situation with no real thoughts or intentions toward marriage. The Jewish Talmud assumes that Tamar was of illegitimate birth, and therefore the two could have been married.

Amnon's "love" was really just lust that, once gratified, turned to hatred (13:15). In thrusting Tamar out of his apartment Amnon was apparently trying to put the blame on her, as if she had seduced him. Tamar's long-sleeved garment (13:18-19) had marked her as a virgin daughter of the king. Upon leaving Amnon's apartment Tamar tore her robe and put ashes (literally, "dust") on her head as an expression of her grief over her humiliation and loss of virginity.

The Slaying of Amnon by Absalom (13:20-29)

When David learned of Amnon's violation of Tamar he was very angry but did nothing to punish his son (13:21). That may be due to the fact that Amnon was David's first-born (3:2) and would be expected to succeed David to the throne. David did not want to carry out the death penalty that Amnon deserved (cf. Lev. 20: 17). Neither did David invoke a lesser disciplinary action (cf. Deut. 22:28-29). Absalom hated Amnon because of the incident but said nothing. He delayed vengeance for two years, perhaps in order to catch Amnon off guard and to carefully plan the murder. With the help of his servants Absalom had Amnon slain during the sheep-shearing festivities at Baal Hazor, a four thousand-foot mountain about twelve miles north of Jerusalem. Absalom's murder of Amnon was probably motivated by two factors: (1) his desire to avenge Tamar's rape, and (2) his desire to enhance his own chance to make a bid for the throne. David's second son, Chileab (3:3), must have died young, for he does not figure at all in the succession narratives. With Amnon dead, Absalom would be next in line for the throne.

The Retreat of Absalom to Geshur (13:30-39)

The first report received by David concerning the events at Baal Hazor was an exaggerated rumor (13:30). Then he learned from Jonadab that only Amnon had been killed (13:32). Although the rest of David's sons returned to Jerusalem (13:34-36), Absalom fled to Geshur (a region in northern Transjordan), where he sought refuge for three years with Talmai, his grandfather (3:3). Verse 39 records that David gradually accepted the fact of Amnon's death and became anxious to see Absalom again. The scene is set for chapter 14 and the return of Absalom.

The Return of Absalom to Jerusalem (14:1-33)

Chapter 14 records how Joab, the commander of David's troops, used a subtle means in helping David see the error of his ways and call Absalom back from Geshur. Three factors probably contributed to Joab's desire to see David and Absalom reconciled: (1) he may have discerned the desire of David's heart (13:39); (2) he may have thought that Absalom had the best chance to succeed David to the throne (3:2-3); and (3) the friction between David and Absalom probably had a demoralizing effect on the army and people of Israel. As had Nathan (12:1-12), Joab took a back-door approach in showing David the error of his ways and encouraging him to call Absalom back to Jerusalem. He sent to Tekoa (Khirbet Tequa, about ten miles south of Jerusalem) for a woman distinguished for her wise dealings. Joab instructed her to pretend to be in mourning and relate a fabricated story to David (14:4-9). The essence of the story is that one brother killed another, and if the death penalty for murder was invoked as other relatives were demanding (cf. Exod. 21:12; Lev. 24:17), then there would be no living heir. That would result in the extinction of the family line, worsening the misfortune.

David apparently wanted to put the woman off, seeking to avoid becoming guilty himself by defending the guilty son. But the persistent woman expressed her willingness to bear any guilt in the place of the king (14:9). He then authorized the woman to bring her persecutors before him for judgment, promising to protect the life of her surviving son (14:10-11). With considerable boldness the woman of Tekoa then applied the principle of David's judgment to his own life and relationship with Absalom (14:13). Verse 14 may be a reflection of Amnon and serve to remind David that the dead cannot be brought back to life, even by punishing the living. The woman suggests that God's will is not to destroy another life, but to bring the banished Absalom home. In verses 15-17 the woman returns to her own case as if to indicate that her concern about the king and Absalom was merely subsidiary.

David quickly recognized Joab's hand in the plan for reconciliation (14:18-20). The woman then "told all" and expressed her confidence in David's wisdom to do what was right. The recall of Absalom from Geshur was immediately arranged, and the king's son was escorted by Joab back to Jerusalem (14:23). However, although Absalom was back in Jerusalem, he was refused an audience with the king (14:24). That evidenced David's unwillingness to completely forgive and bore bitter fruit in the heart of Absalom. Verses 25-27 are parenthetical and present Absalom as an attractive prince who could easily win the hearts of the people of Israel (cf. 15:1-6). According to verse 26, his head produced approximately three and a half pounds of hair annually.

The chapter concludes by recording the reconciliation between David and Absalom (14:28-33). Absalom had to burn Joab's field to get any action on the matter, but after living in Jerusalem two full years he was restored to favor with David (14:33). But the seed of bitterness had been sown, and for two years Absalom had nourished it in the anger of his heart. The seed would soon bear the fruit of conspiracy and rebellion against his father David.

ABSALOM'S REBELLION (15:1—18:33)

Being shunned by David for two full years in Jerusalem caused Absalom to grow bitter. That bitter resentment eventuated in rebellion against his father the king. Chapters 15-18 record how David was forced to flee Jerusalem as Absalom usurped the throne.

The Conspiracy of Absalom (15:1-12)

Absalom spent four years quietly laying plans for his rebellion. His strategy included: (1) the elevation of himself through pomp and ceremony (15:1); (2) criticism of his father's administration of justice (15:2-3); (3) boastful "campaign promises" (15:4); and (4) personal charm and flattery (15:5-6). Absalom's rebellion began in Hebron, where David had been initially recognized as king (2:1-4). There Absalom had more freedom in instigating rebellion away from the watchful eye of his father in Jerusalem. At Hebron Absalom may have found supporters who begrudged David for moving the capital to Jerusalem. The "forty years" of verse 7 is probably a scribal error in transmission and should read "four years" according to the Septuagint, Syriac, and Josephus (*Antiquities* VII. 196). The number "forty" could refer neither to the age of Absalom or the year of David's reign, for Absalom was born at Hebron after David had begun to reign, and David reigned only forty years in all. The rebellion could not have taken place in the last weeks of his reign. The four-year period began either with Absalom's return from Geshur (14:23) or his reconciliation with David (14:33).

Absalom found his initial partisans in two hundred unsuspecting men who joined him in Hebron for the supposed fulfillment of his vow (15:7-8, 11). While marshalling his support in Hebron, Absalom directed certain co-conspirators to prepare to announce his kingship throughout Israel (15:10). Absalom also found a supporter in Ahithophel, David's counselor and Bathsheba's grandfather (11:3, 23:34), who may have resented David's treatment of his granddaughter (15:12). The conspiracy of Absalom was in full swing by the time David received word that anything was amiss.

The Flight of David from Jerusalem (15:13—16:14)

When David learned of Absalom's revolt, he fled from Jerusalem. Verse 14 reveals why. David feared for his life and the destruction of Jerusalem should he remain in the city. Perhaps he was also seeking to avert civil war and bloodshed by stepping aside. David must have expected (or hoped) to return to Jerusalem, for he left ten concubines there to keep house (15:16). David's servants and royal guard demonstrated their loyalty to the king by following him into exile (15:15-18). Included in that contingent of followers was a group of six hundred soldiers from Gath (probably Philistines) who evidently served as mercenary soldiers for the king.

The loyalty of Ittai the Gittite (i.e., formerly of Gath) is reminiscent of Ruth's loyalty to Naomi (15:19-23; Ruth 1:15-18). David's comment in verse 19 does not imply that he recognized Absalom as king, but he was simply encouraging Ittai to remain in Jerusalem with whomever God should appoint to rule Israel (cf. 15:25-26). Ittai's later appointment as commander of one-third of the army (18:2) was David's way of expressing appreciation for that demonstration of loyalty.

After crossing the brook Kidron east of the city, David noticed that Zadok and Abiathar were bringing the Ark out of Jerusalem. David commanded that the Ark be returned to the city, committing the whole situation to the Lord to work out His sovereign will

(15:25-26). He further instructed Zadok and Abiathar to remain in Jerusalem with the Ark and to gather information for him as to what was going on in the capital during Absalom's revolt (15:28-29, 35-36). Through their sons they would relay reports to David concerning developments in Jerusalem. David not only arranged for those intelligence operations in Jerusalem, but also appointed his faithful servant Hushai to thwart the counsel that disloyal Ahithophel gave Absalom (15:31-34). In addition, Hushai was given the decisive role of relaying official classified information to the priests, whose sons would then inform David.

Passing a short distance beyond the summit of the Mount of Olives David encountered Ziba (cf. 9:2-13), the servant of Jonathan's crippled son Mephibosheth. Ziba graciously brought provisions for David and his men, but accused Mephibosheth of disloyalty (16:1-3). Ziba's accusation against his master is seen in 19:24-28 to be false. He was evidently trying to commend himself in the eyes of David and temporarily succeeded (16:4).

When David came to Bahurim (perhaps Ras el-Temim) near the edge of the wilderness of Judah he was met by Shimei, a distant relative of Saul. Shimei cursed the departing king, describing him as a "man of bloodshed" (16:7). He declared that the loss of the throne was God's retribution on David's past sins (16:8). That seemed credible enough to David, who took Shimei's curse as from the Lord (16:11). Hence, David refused to allow Abishai to "cut off his head" (16:9). David's words to Abishai in verse 10, "What have I to do with you?" suggests the idea that their attitudes toward the situation were totally different. After a long march through the wilderness David and his band of followers arrived at the Jordan and refreshed themselves there before crossing over to Transjordan enroute to Mahanaim (17:24).

The Counsel of Ahithophel and Hushai (16:15–17:23)

By leaving a few faithful followers in Jerusalem, David was able to nullify the counsel that Ahithophel gave Absalom. When Absalom came to Jerusalem he was greeted by David's loyal friend, Hushai, who pretended to give his allegiance to the usurper (16:15-19). His special "ministry" in Absalom's court was to "thwart the counsel of Ahithophel" for David's benefit (15:34).

Ahithophel's first bit of advice to Absalom was for him to appropriate his father's concubines (16:21). In ancient times the seizure of the royal harem demonstrated possession of the throne (cf. 3:7). That action would remove any possibility of reconciliation between David and Absalom. Since the counsel of Ahithophel was regarded as if it was the very "word of God" (16:23), the advice was well received. The public spectacle that followed was the greatest possible insult that Absalom could fling at David (16:22; cf. Lev. 18:8).

Ahithophel further counseled that David and his followers should be immediately pursued and killed to remove any possibility of their reclaiming the throne (17:1-2). It was suggested that David's followers would probably return to Absalom if the exiled king were killed (17:3). God then used Hushai, David's loyal friend, to thwart the counsel of Ahithophel and lead Absalom to his death (17:14). Hushai first criticized the advice of Ahithophel and then with eloquence and flattery warned against attacking David at that time since he was such an expert at warfare. He also advised Absalom to first organize the army and then personally lead his troops into battle (7:7-8, 11).

David was quickly informed of Absalom's decision through the exiled king's official intelligence channel (cf. 15:30-37). Hushai reported the developments to Zadok and Abiathar (priests) who relayed the news to David by way of their sons, Jonathan and Ahimaaz. The priests' sons barely escaped being apprehended by Absalom's servants (16:17-20) but successfully reported the developments in Jerusalem to David (16:21-22). When Ahithophel saw that his counsel to Absalom had not been followed, he took his own life. Two factors probably contributed to his suicide: (1) he was humiliated by the rejection of his advice, and (2) he could probably foresee Absalom's defeat and knew that he would then be accountable to David for his disloyalty.

The Defeat of Absalom's Army (17:24–18:8)

Receiving word of Absalom's plans, David and his followers crossed over the Jordan and came to Mahanaim, Ish-bosheth's former capital in Transjordan (2:8; 17:24). He was pursued by Absalom and his army, which had been placed under the command of

Amasa, Joab's temporary successor. While in exile, Shobi, David's vassal in Ammon (8:12; 10:1-4), and other rulers in Transjordan graciously provided for the physical needs of David and his men (17:27-29).

To prepare for battle David counted and reviewed his fighting forces (18:1). He then divided his men into three companies—a frequent military maneuver in antiquity (Judg. 7:16; 1 Sam. 11:11; 13:7). Although David wanted to lead his men in battle, he was persuaded to remain at Mahanaim, both for his protection and to defend the city (18:3-4). As the army moved out for battle David commanded his generals to "deal gently" with Absalom, apparently viewing the rebellion of Absalom as a youthful escapade that could be forgiven. Joab and the army regarded the rebellion as having much more serious consequences. The battle took place in the forest of Ephraim—a dense forest north of the Jabbok River in Transjordan. The newly organized army of Absalom was no match for the seasoned soldiers of David, and twenty thousand of Absalom's men were killed (18:6-7). Because of the rugged nature of the terrain, the pursuit through the forest resulted in more deaths than did the actual combat (18:8).

The Death of Absalom (18:9-18)

The tradition that Absalom was caught by his hair actually comes from Josephus (*Antiquities* VII. 239), but it makes good sense in light of 14:26. When the report of Absalom's predicament came to Joab, he reproved the warrior for not putting him to death (18:11). Joab was a ruthless military leader who viewed Absalom not so much as David's son but as David's enemy who had usurped the throne. In disobedience to the explicit orders of David, Joab took the life of the king's son Absalom (18:5, 14-15). The death of Absalom meant an end to the revolt, and so Joab called a halt to the pursuit of the rebels. Absalom was buried in a deep pit that was then covered over with stones, perhaps symbolic of stoning that was the legal penalty due to a rebel son (cf. Deut. 21:20-21).

The Report of Victory and Absalom's Death (18:19-33)

The rest of chapter 18 records the report of some good news and some bad news to David—Joab's victory and Absalom's death.

Ahimaaz, the son of Zadok, wanted to report the victory to the king, but Joab wanted the Cushite slave to deliver the report in case David reacted violently to the news of his son's death. Ahimaaz was persistent and finally got permission from Joab to deliver the message (18:23). When David saw the Cushite runner approaching he predicted a message of good news (18:25). Perhaps a band of men running toward the city would indicate a rout, but one man, a victory. Ahimaaz outran the Cushite slave and reported the victory to David (18:28). When David questioned him about Absalom, Ahimaaz feigned ignorance. He was lying, for Joab had told him explicitly that the king's son was dead (18:20). It was the slave runner who delivered the report of Absalom's death to David. Verse 33 record's David's sad lament for his rebel son. The tragedy of Absalom was one of the consequences of David's sin with Bathsheba (12:11-12). Although David's sin was forgiven, he still reaped its inevitable and unhappy consequences in his life.

DAVID'S REINSTATEMENT AS KING (19:1—20:26)

Chapters 19-20 record how Judah and Israel became reunited and brought David back to Jerusalem as king. Those chapters also tell of another rather short-lived rebellion against David led by a Benjamite named Sheba.

Judah Calls David Back as King (19:1-14)

David's unrestrained grief over Absalom's death could have led to political disaster. Because of David's grief the warriors returned from battle not as rejoicing victors, but as those humiliated by defeat (19:3). Recognizing that potentially disastrous situation, Joab took bold steps to rebuke the king for failing to appreciate the victory that his men had won for him. Joab warned David that his disposition was having a negative effect on the morale and loyalty of his followers and that he would be in deep trouble if he did not immediately express appreciation to his men for their victory (19:7). David recognized the wisdom of Joab's counsel and went to the city gate to address his faithful followers. Verse 8 notes parenthetically that "Israel had fled"—that is, the followers of Absalom had returned home.

The movement to restore David to power was not at first unanimous. Some Israelites evidently thought he had lost his right to rule. Others looked upon him as having earned his right to rule by his past service for the nation (19:9). It was finally recognized that since Absalom was dead, David ought to be reinstated as king. Verse 11 indicates that the elders of Judah were reticent to invite David to return, perhaps because of the part they played in Absalom's insurrection (cf. 15:10-11). David fully recognized the need for the support of his own tribe and sought to encourage their allegiance. Note in verse 13 that David replaced his commander Joab with Amasa, the commander of Absalom's army (cf. 17:25). That move was designed to (1) secure the allegiance of the rebel army, and (2) discipline Joab for slaying Absalom (cf. 18:14-15). David's diplomacy was effective in securing an invitation from the people of Judah to return as king (19:14).

David Met by His Supporters (19:15-40)

Returning to Jerusalem from exile David was met at the Jordan by his friends and supporters from both Israel and Judah. Among those who went out to meet David was Shimei, who had cursed David as he had fled Jerusalem during Absalom's revolt (cf. 16:5-8). Shimei confessed his sin, and his life was spared—at least temporarily. The amnesty granted Shimei by David was apparently only temporary or conditioned on continued loyalty, for on his deathbed the king ordered that Shimei be punished for his crime (cf. 1 Kings 2:8-9, 36-46). In verse 20 the expression "house of Joseph" is a reference to Ephraim (the offspring of Joseph's son), a large tribe of Israel and was representative of the ten northern tribes.

Mephibosheth, Jonathan's crippled son, also met David at the Jordan and exhibited the traditional marks of mourning (19:24). He had been in that condition since the king's departure. Mephibosheth explained that he had not followed David into exile because he had been deceived by his servant Ziba (19:26). It is surprising that David rebuffed Mephibosheth and decided to divide Saul's land between Ziba and Mephibosheth. There are at least three possible explanations for that decision: (1) David did not believe that Mephibosheth was totally innocent (16:3); (2) David was trying to repay Ziba for his kindness (16:1-4) and just forgave the deceit or; (3) David did not take the time to hear the case and simply made a poor judgment.

Before crossing the Jordan back into Judah, David said farewell to his faithful friend Barzillai who had provided for his needs at Mahanaim during his exile (19:31-32). David offered to let Barzillai live in Jerusalem as his guest, but his friend preferred to live out his last years in his own house (19:33-39). As David journeyed from the Jordan to Gilgal on his way to Jerusalem he had the full support of Judah, but only half the people of Israel came out to show their support for his rule. Another insurrection was in the making.

Sheba's Rebellion Suppressed by Joab (19:41—20:22)

Quarreling soon broke out between the northern tribes of Israel and the people of Judah. The men of Israel were annoyed by the fact that David's supporters in Judah made it to the Jordan and helped the king cross over without sharing the privilege with them (19:41-43). The harsh words that were exchanged between the men of Israel and Judah were an evidence of the discontent that gave rise to Sheba's rebellion.

It was Sheba, of the tribe of Benjamin, who called the men of Israel to revolt. His "campaign slogan" was, "every man to his tents" (20:1)—that is, "Let's go home and from there we will resist the king." David quickly lost the little support he had enjoyed from the northern tribes (20:2). Verse 3 notes parenthetically that when David returned to Jerusalem he shut up his ten concubines to a life of widowhood because of their sexual relations with Absalom (cf. 16:21-22).

The military record of Amasa, who replaced Joab, was not one to inspire confidence (cf. 18:6-18). His slowness in carrying out David's order to organize the troops to deal with Sheba's revolt could have resulted in another disaster, so Joab saw to his slaying (20:4-10). Taking hold of one's beard and kissing the cheek was a customary Oriental greeting. Joab used the greeting to put Amasa off guard while he raised his sword for the fatal thrust.

The command of David's army was transferred again to Joab, who pursued Sheba to Abel Beth-maacah (Abil el-Qamh) about twenty-five miles north of the Sea of Galilee (20:13-15). While

Abel Beth-maacah was under siege, a wise woman of the city questioned Joab as to why he would destroy "a mother in Israel" (i.e., a mother city or recognized capital of the region). She also questioned Joab's failure to offer the citizens terms of peace in accordance with the provisions of Deuteronomy 20:11. Persuaded that the death of Sheba would end the siege, the people cut off his head and threw it over the wall to Joab. The revolt was over with the death of Sheba, and so the troops dispersed and returned home (20:22). David's rule was now secure both in Israel and Judah.

David's Chief Officers (20:23-26)

The chapter concludes with a reference to David's chief officers. It is interesting to compare this list of officers with the earlier record of 8:15-18. The name *Adoram* is rendered "Adoniram" in 1 Kings 4:6, 28. The forced labor that Adoram supervised (20:24) was one of the evils of kingship that had been promised by Samuel (1 Sam. 8:11-16).

6

THE APPENDIX TO DAVID'S CAREER

2 SAMUEL 21-24

THE GIBEONITES AVENGED FOR THE BROKEN TREATY (21:1-14)
THE EXPLOITS OF DAVID AND HIS MEN (21:15-22)
THE PSALM OF DECLARATIVE PRAISE FOR DELIVERANCE (22:1-51)
THE LAST WORDS OF DAVID (23:1-7)
THE ROSTER OF DAVID'S MIGHTY MEN (23:8-39)
THE NUMBERING OF THE PEOPLE AND THE PESTILENCE (24:1-25)

6

THE APPENDIX TO DAVID'S CAREER

2 SAMUEL 21-24

The last chapters of 2 Samuel serve as an appendix to David's career. Several of the events recorded or referred to in these chapters occurred earlier in David's life but are presented here to show the other kinds of problems that David had to face—famine and plague (21, 24)—and how David learned to praise God through his trials (22). The section concludes with David's purchase of the site upon which Solomon would later build the Temple.

THE GIBEONITES AVENGED FOR THE BROKEN TREATY (21:1-14)

The first part of chapter 21 records God's judgment on Israel for breaking the treaty with the Gibeonites (Josh. 9:1). Since the events of chapter 9 and the reasons for Shimei's cursing (16:7-8) presuppose the execution of the seven descendants of Saul, it may be concluded that the events of this chapter fit better at the beginning of David's reign. However, although these events are out of order chronologically, they fit well topically since, like chapters 19 and 20, they focus on David's dealings with Saul's supporters and descendants.

When Israel experienced three years of famine David began to recognize it as divine chastening (cf. Deut. 28:47-48) and sought God for the reason. By divine revelation he learned that a sin had been committed by "Saul and his bloody house" (21:1). In his zeal to exterminate the heathen from Israel Saul had slain some of the Gibeonites with whom Israel had made a treaty some four hundred years earlier (cf. Josh. 9:3-27). When David asked the Gibeonites what they would accept as settlement for the wrong done, they demanded justice in keeping with the principle of Numbers

124 FIRST AND SECOND SAMUEL

35:31—a life demands a life. David consented to allow the Gibeonites to execute seven of Saul's descendants. The word *son* (20:6) can mean son, grandson, or descendant. The word *hang* in 21:6 is too specific a term. In the original, the word suggests some form of solemn execution involving the exposure of the dead body (cf. Num. 25:4). Exposing a corpse to public view was considered a great dishonor for the dead and added humiliation to the death penalty.

David spared Mephibosheth, the son of Jonathan and grandson of Saul, on account of their covenant of friendship (cf. 1 Sam. 18:3; 20:8, 16) and delivered up two sons of Rizpah, Saul's concubine, and five sons of Merab, Saul's daughter. Note that the Mephibosheth of verse 7 is Jonathan's son who was spared and is distinct from the son of Rizpah, by the same ñame (21:8), who was executed. The name *Michal*, which occurs in verse 8 of the King James Version and some Hebrew manuscripts probably represents a scribal error in transmission for Merab who was the wife of Adriel (cf. 1 Sam. 18:19; 2 Sam. 6:23). That view is supported by several Hebrew manuscripts and the Septuagint.

Since the Old Testament explicitly prohibited the punishment of a son for the sins of his father (cf. Deut. 24:16; 2 Kings 14:6; Ezek. 18:1-4, 14-17) this passage presents us with a moral problem. How could David rightly punish those men for the sins of Saul? Perhaps David did wrong. Yet there is no condemnation of David in the text, and God apparently honored the action taken and ended the famine (21:4). Perhaps it is better to understand that the seven descendants of Saul who were executed had been implicated in the killing of the Gibeonites. That explanation is suggested in verse 1 by the phrase, "It is for Saul and his *bloody house*" (italics added).

Grief-stricken, Rizpah remained by the bodies from the barley harvest in April to the early rains in October, protecting the dead from scavengers (21:10-11). According to Old Testament law the bodies should have been buried on the same day as the execution and not left overnight (Deut. 21:22-23). Later David retrieved the bones of Saul and Jonathan and buried them at Zela (either an unidentified site or a tomb in the territory of Benjamin) with the bodies of the men who had been executed. Although 1 Samuel

31:12 records that the men of Jabesh took the bodies of Saul and
Jonathan from the wall of Beth-shan, here it is stated that they
were retrieved from the open square. Apparently the bodies were
taken from the wall situated by the open square of the city. In due
time the famine ended, and God restored the land to prosperity.

THE EXPLOITS OF DAVID AND HIS MEN (21:15-22)

The rest of chapter 21 records the exploits of David and his men
against the Philistine giants. The point of the record is that David
was delivered from four great foes. That theme of deliverance
prepares the reader for the psalm recorded in chapter 22. The Hebrew word translated "giant" (21:16, 18, 20, 22) is literally *raphah*.
It is not the name of an individual but is a term used collectively
for the Rephaim who inhabited the land of Canaan in early times
and were noted for their inordinate size (cf. Gen. 15:19-21; Deut.
2:11, 3:11, 13; Num. 13:33).

David's faithful soldier, Abishai, is noted to have slain the
Philistine giant Ishbi-benob, whose spear weighed approximately
seven and a half pounds (21:15-17). The "lamp of Israel" (21:
17) refers to David, whose life and actions were as a light kindled
for Israel. The Philistine giant Saph was slain by Sibbecai the
Hushathite (21:18). The Hebrew text of verse 19 attributes the
slaying of Goliath to Elhanan in contradiction with the account of
David's victory recorded in 1 Sam. 17:50. There are at least three
possible solutions to this problem. First, there could have been two
giants named Goliath. Second, Elhanan and David may be different names for the same person, just as Solomon had another name
(2 Sam. 12:24-25). Third, there has been a scribal error in transmission and the text should read, "Elhanan . . . killed the *brother*
of Goliath." That third view is supported by the parallel account
in 1 Chronicles 20:5. The last giant mentioned is not named but
was noted for his twelve toes as well as his size (21:20-22). He
was killed by David's nephew Jonathan, the son of Shimei (also
called Shammah in 1 Sam. 16:9).

THE PSALM OF DECLARATIVE PRAISE FOR
DELIVERANCE (22:1-51)

The hymn of praise recorded in chapter 22 is almost identical to

Psalm 18. This psalm serves as a theological commentary on the life of David, pointing to the fact that the victories and successes he enjoyed were due to Yahweh's intervention and enablement. The psalm records David's response to God's goodness in delivering him from his enemies and particularly from King Saul. To *praise* God essentially means to *confess* Him publicly or give public acknowledgment concerning God's character or His activity. There are two categories of praise in the psalms: (1) descriptive praise; and (2) declarative praise. Descriptive praise focuses on what God is like (His attributes). Declarative praise emphasizes what God has done (His actions). The psalm recorded here is of the latter category. It is a psalm of declarative praise of the individual for what God has accomplished in the life of David.

This psalm was occasioned by God's deliverance of David from Saul during his wilderness exploits. Possibly the psalm is based on the historical incident recorded in 1 Sam. 23:24-28. After the deliverance David wrote a song to give public acknowledgment of God's goodness to him. That psalm testimony focuses not on David, the delivered, but on God, the deliverer. In verses 2-4 David began praising God for His deliverance. The expression, "horn of salvation" (22:3), is a figure borrowed from the concept of animal horns, which were used both for protection and defense. Verse 4 is actually an introductory summary of the message of the psalm. David stated that God is worthy of praise for He had delivered him.

David went on in verses 5 and 6 to reflect on the circumstances in which he almost lost his life. Then he reported God's deliverance (22:7-19). In verses 8-15 the appearance of God ("epiphany of God") to deliver is described in terms reminiscent of His appearance to Moses at Mt. Sinai—with earthquakes, thunder, darkness, and lightning. David recalled that as Yahweh delivered Israel from the Egyptians, so He had delivered David from his enemies (22:16-19).

The reasons for Yahweh's condescension and deliverance are recorded in verses 20-28. There are six: (1) God delighted in David, v. 20; (2) David was righteous, vv. 21, 25; (3) David was obedient to God's law, vv. 22-23; (4) David kept himself from iniquity, v. 24; (5) God is loyal to those loyal to Him, vv. 26-27; and (6) God saves the afflicted (David) and humbles the proud (Saul), v. 28.

The next section of the psalm describes what David could do by the Lord's enablement (22:29-40). This is the Philippians 4:13 of the Old Testament, "I can do all things through Him who strengthens me." David concludes his psalm of thanksgiving with renewed praise for God's glorious deeds (22:47-51). God is likened to a rock (22:47). He is strong, steadfast, and a place of refuge. Because God delivers His own (22:48-49), David vowed to praise Him (22:50). He concluded the psalm by doing so (22:51).

THE LAST WORDS OF DAVID (23:1-7)

David's "last words" (23:1) probably represent his last formal utterance before his death. This last psalm of David expresses praise to God, the righteous ruler and covenant keeper. In verse 1 David is introduced as the "sweet psalmist of Israel." Of the 150 psalms in the Hebrew psalter, seventy-three are attributed to David. The divine inspiration of his poetic compositions is suggested in verse 2, "The Spirit of the LORD spoke by me, and His word was on my tongue." The doctrine of the inspiration of Scripture is developed in 2 Timothy 3:16-17; 2 Peter 1:20-21; and Acts 4:25. Verses 3-5 form the central core of the psalm. There David expressed his faith that God would consummate the "everlasting covenant" that He established in 2 Samuel 7:12-16. The ultimate fulfillment of the covenant provisions will take place at the second coming, when Christ returns to reign over David's kingdom (cf. Luke 1:31-33). In concluding the psalm David anticipated the divine judgment of Yahweh upon the ungodly who dare to persecute Abraham's descendants. David had confidence that God will fulfill His promise to the patriarch in cursing those who curse Israel (cf. Gen. 12:3; Zech. 2:8-9).

THE ROSTER OF DAVID'S MIGHTY MEN (23:8-39)

The rest of chapter 23 commemorates the names and achievements of thirty-seven of David's bravest warriors. First Chronicles 11:10 reveals that those men gave David their strong support and helped him become king. The phrase "mighty men" suggests that those were the elite of David's troops (cf. 1 Sam. 22:2) and may have served as his bodyguard. The first three mentioned distinguished themselves in the wars against the Philistines (23:8-11). Each is acknowledged for having single-handedly killed a great number of the enemy during battles Israel would have otherwise lost.

The episode recorded in 23:13-17 tells of the feat of the "three" who broke through the Philistine battlelines to get water for David from the well of Bethlehem. Some would identify the "three" as those mentioned in 23:8-12, but the writer clearly intends to leave them anonymous. The story reflects the sacrificial commitment David's men demonstrated in his behalf. They were willing to risk their lives to satisfy his wishes. David's men brought him the water from Bethlehem's well at the risk of their own lives. Therefore David considered it as "blood" and refused to drink it (23:17; cf. Lev. 17:11). Instead, he poured it out on the ground as a sacrifice to Yahweh (cf. Gen. 35:14; Exod. 30:9; Lev. 23:13, 18, 37).

Next, the single-handed feats of Abishai and Benaiah are commemorated (23:18-23). The number *three* recorded in the KJV of verse 18 probably represents a scribal error in transmission. The better reading is "thirty" in keeping with two Hebrew manuscripts, the Syriac, and the context of 23:17-19. Benaiah is noted to have killed "the two Ariel of Moab" (v. 20). The Hebrew word *Ariel* literally means "lion of God" and may be a metaphor for "military champions" rather than a personal name.

Apparently the *thirty* (23:24) represents an elite core of David's mighty men, and the military unit was added to as men were killed. Hence, although the list in verses 24-39 contains more than thirty men, the number of active soldiers in this special unit was probably kept at thirty. The *thirty-seven* mentioned in verse 39 includes the three (23:8-12), Abishai and Benaiah (23:18-23), the thirty-one warriors (23:24-39), and David's commander, Joab (23:37).

THE NUMBERING OF THE PEOPLE AND THE PESTILENCE (24:1-25)

Numbering the people in ancient times was usually done for purposes of determining taxes or drafting men into the military (cf. Luke 2:1-3; Num. 1:2-3). David's numbering of the people is recorded here because it forms the historical background for the events that led David to buy the site upon which the Temple would be built. What motivated David to number the people? Verse 1 indicates that he was prompted by Yahweh's anger, whereas 1 Chronicles 21:1 reveals that he was prompted by Satan. The two accounts reflect two aspects of the same incident. Although Satan actually instigated the pride and rebellion that led to the numbering of the people, God permitted Satan to exercise that influence so that His divine plan might be carried out (cf. Gen. 50:20). Although Joab protested the plan, he was overruled by David. After nine months and twenty days of census taking, Joab presented the king with the official figures—eight hundred thousand adult males in Israel and five hundred thousand in Judah. Verse 9 suggests that David's census was for military purposes. It was the first step necessary in preparing to draft an army.

After the numbering, David recognized and confessed his sin. Why was that numbering considered sinful when God had commanded a similar census earlier in Israel's history (cf. Num. 1: 1-3)? Josephus speculates that David's error was in forgetting to collect the half shekel for every head counted (cf. Exod. 30:12-13; *Antiquities* VII. 318). It is also possible that David had been commanded not to number the people but did so anyway. Perhaps the sin was David's own lack of faith in God's protective care over the nation. He may have been trusting in himself and the military strength he could muster rather than in the Lord. David fell into deep sin on several occasions; but his heart was sensitive, and he was always quick to confess his wrong and seek restoration.

David was given a choice of three possible punishments for his sin of numbering the people (24:13). The choices included: (1) seven years of famine for Israel; (2) three months of fleeing from the enemy; or (3) three days of pestilence in the land. The choices move to increasing severity with a diminishing duration. David knew that God would be more merciful than his enemies and apparently took the third option (24:14). Yahweh sent pestilence on the land, which resulted in the deaths of seventy thousand Israelites. However, the judgment was stopped by Yahweh before it reached Jerusalem (24:16). The expression *relented* (or "repented," KJV) is not an indication of changeability in God's character (1 Sam. 15:29; James 1:17), but an expression of His deep sorrow concerning man's sin and evil.

The rest of the chapter records how David purchased the threshing floor of Araunah (known as Ornan in 2 Chron. 3:1), erected an altar, and made an offering in order to stop the plague. Although Araunah wanted to *give* David the threshing floor and oxen for sacrifice, David did not want to offer to the Lord that which cost him nothing (24:24). David gave *sacrificially* to the Lord—a principle of giving that the New Testament commends (2 Cor. 8:1-3). The pestilence was actually checked by Yahweh's mercy (24:16), unbeknown to David, before he bought the threshing floor and presented his offering to the Lord. However, the purchase of the threshing floor is detailed because of its future significance in Israel's worship. On that site Solomon would later build the Temple. The site is identified in 2 Chron. 3:1 as Mount Moriah—traditionally the hill in the land of Moriah where Abraham offered Isaac for sacrifice (Gen. 22:2). The preservation of Jerusalem (24:16) and the purchase of the Temple site (24:24) prepare the way for the advent of David's successor, Solomon.

BIBLIOGRAPHY

Bright, John. *A History of Israel*. 2nd ed. Philadelphia: Westminster, 1972.

Crockett, William Day. *A Harmony of Samuel, Kings and Chronicles*. Grand Rapids: Baker, 1951.

Davis, John J. *The Birth of a Kingdom*. Winona Lake, Ind.: BMH Books, 1970.

Driver, S. R. *Notes on the Hebrew Text and the Topography of the Books of Samuel*. 2nd ed. Oxford: Clarendon, 1913.

Goldman, S. Samuel. *Soncino Books of the Bible*. London: Soncino, 1951.

Hertzberg, Hans Wilhelm. *I and II Samuel*. Translated by J. S. Bowden. Philadelphia: Westminster, 1964.

Keil, C. F., and Delitzsch, F. *The Books of Samuel*. Translated by James Martin. Edinburgh: T. & T. Clark, 1872.

Kirkpatrick, A. F. *I, II Samuel*. The Cambridge Bible for Schools and Colleges. Cambridge: Cambridge U., 1930.

Mauchline, John. *1 and 2 Samuel*. New Century Bible. Greenwood, S.C.: Attic, 1971.

Merrill, Eugene H. *An Historical Survey of the Old Testament*. Nutley, N.J.: Craig, 1966.

Payne, D. F. "1 and 2 Samuel." In *The New Bible Commentary: Revised*. Edited by D. Guthrie and J. A. Motyer. Grand Rapids: Eerdmans, 1970.

Smith, H. P. *Samuel*. International Critical Commentary. Edinburgh: T. & T. Clark, 1899.

Wood, Leon. *A Survey of Israel's History*. Grand Rapids: Zondervan, 1970.

Young, Fred E. "First and Second Samuel." In *The Wycliffe Bible Commentary*. Edited by Charles F. Pfeiffer and Everett F. Harrison. Chicago: Moody, 1962.